How To Be A

Victorious

CHRISTIAN

How To Be A

Victorious

CHRISTIAN

Thomas A. Davis

P. O. Box 449
Ukiah, CA 95482
800-471-4284

ACKNOWLEDGMENTS

The quotation from *The Gospel of John*, vol. 2, by William Barclay (pp. 37, 38), is from *The Daily Study Bible*, published by the Saint Andrew Press, Edinburgh, Scotland. Quoted by permission.

The texts from *The New American Standard Bible*, copyright © The Lockman Foundadon 1960, 1962, 1963, 1971, 1973 are used by permission.

Excerpt from *The Jerusalem Bible*, copyright © 1966 by Dayton, Longman & Todd, Ltd. and Doubleday & Company, Inc. Used by permission of the publishers.

The texts from *Today's English Version of the New Testament*, copyright © American Bible Society 1966. Used by permission.

Cover Design by Greg Solie - Altamont Graphics

Some images © 2003 www.clipart.com

ISBN 0-9659327-9-6

Foreword

The greatest need of the Seventh-day Adventist Church today is not more money, bigger budgets, more buildings, more institutions and facilities. It is not even more evangelistic crusades. What we as Seventh-day Adventist Church members need is *to be saved from our sins*. God is not waiting for more storms, more political furor, more wars and rumors of wars, before Jesus can come. He is waiting for His people to gain the victory over sin, so that He can trust them with heaven. Jesus came "to save his people from their sins"; to help us to be overcomers!

That we might understand how this may be is the reason for the writing of this book; for *How to Be a Victorious Christian*, by Thomas A. Davis, deals with the practice of the Christian faith. In a simple, yet forceful, manner he places before his readers the way to live the Christian life as a true overcomer. Step by step he makes the way inviting and very practical. Jesus will live again in your experience as you see Him lifted up in all His beauty and loveliness in every page.

ROBERT H. PIERSON
President
General Conference of Seventh-day
Adventists

Contents

8

Perspective and Objective

VICTORY, victory in Christ, is what the Christian life is all about. Victory over any and every sin, every weakness, every failing, that is in the life.

But many Seventh-day Adventists are conscious that they are not having complete victory in their lives. An informal survey recently conducted in one large Adventist church revealed that a sizable majority of the members were unsure of their relationship with Christ. This is not an indication of victory.

I have known defeat in my Christian life. Long years of defeat. By defeat I do not mean temporary setbacks. I mean defeat, time and time again, in my struggle with sin.

Briefly, my story is this: Baptized at 18, sincere in my desire to be a Christian, nevertheless I soon discovered my prebaptism weaknesses were still plaguing me. In spite of myself, I was weak in moral power, plagued by doubts, and under the control of inherited and cultivated leanings to sin. Not sins as the world would count them, perhaps, but sins as God and I knew them to be.

My spiritual life in academy was a teeter-totter one. Fall and spring Weeks of Prayer frequently inspired me to holier living. But soon I would slip back to my old life of doubt and defeat.

During World War II I joined the Royal Canadian Air

Force and spent some two years in England attached to a Canadian bomber squadron as a medic.

Following the war I went back to college; my goal, the ministry. In college I led a fairly active life as a theology student. I preached sermons at the college and nearby churches. I participated in public evangelistic meetings. I gave Bible studies.

Something Lacking

But there still was something lacking in my religious life. Outwardly I was probably what a ministerial student was expected to be. Inwardly there was an unlovely harem of feelings and attitudes—envy, jealousy, self-seeking, pride, un-Christlike ambition—that did not diminish with time, and that I could no more get rid of than I could change the shape of my ears or the color of my eyes.

In time I graduated and was called into the ministry. I served in several pastorates. I gave many Bible studies on the doctrines taught by Seventh-day Adventists. But I could not lead a person to Christ. I could not because I did not really know Him myself. Only a person who truly knows Jesus can lead others to Him.

Meanwhile I married. In my opinion there is nothing more calculated to expose a person's character than marriage. And especially does true character emerge when children come into the home.

With children, problems began to develop in our house. For example, my wife and I would have differences of opinion regarding how the children ought to be handled on various occasions. Sometimes there would be arguments. Afterward, I would go to my knees and ask for forgiveness and victory. And in a few days my wife and I would repeat our past performance. It was a merry-go-round we couldn't get off.

The Turning Point

The turning point came the year we returned home after spending ten years in the mission field. My wife went to visit her parents and some of her brothers and sisters. She returned with a vision. She had seen in one of her sisters a spiritual glow, love, faith, an openness, hopefulness, and Christian victory that she felt she had to have.

She began to search for a deeper life in Christ and to try to share her findings with me. The story of my resistings, and of my finally admitting to myself that pride and self-importance was the reason for my attitude, cannot be told here. What is important is that I finally began to follow some formulas and claim some promises. When I did, I began to discover something about how a person may have real victories in his Christian life.

Which brings us to the objective of this book.

As the title tells us, this volume is intended to be a "how-to" book. It is intended, hopefully, to fulfill to some degree Ellen White's words, "What the people want is instruction. What shall I do that I may save my soul?"— *Counsels to Writers and Editors,* p. 25. I hasten to add, it is not a "do-it-yourself" book, for Christianity is not a "do-it-yourself" religion.

While this is emphatically so, it is just as emphatically not a "do-nothing" religion. "The work of gaining salvation is one of copartnership, a joint operation. There is to be co-operation between God and the repentant sinner."— *The Acts of the Apostles,* p. 482.

Cooperation suggests a plan accepted by the parties involved. Ellen White puts cooperation on a high level when she suggests there is a science to the plan of salvation. "The Bible contains the science of salvation for all those who will hear and do the words of Christ."—*Fundamentals of Christian Education,* p. 187.

In context, the term science suggests there are established principles in Christianity that may be discovered and understood, and that, being faithfully adhered to, will result in freedom from sin, and finally the reality of eternal life. This is further suggested in the familiar words of the Bible: "All scripture is inspired by God and profitable for teaching, for reproof, for correction, and for training in righteousness, that the man of God may be complete, equipped for every good work" (2 Tim. 3:16, 17, R.S.V.).

How to Be a Victorious Christian

an effortless often unconscious assimilation ## Not by Spiritual Osmosis

Salvation, then, is not obtained by some sort of spiritual osmosis, or because God is very gracious and reluctant to destroy sinners—which is, of course, true—but because the sinner cooperates with certain spiritual principles. *chance*

This joint cooperation is not a haphazard, hit-or-miss, accidentally accomplished enterprise. The road to heaven is not discovered, or continued upon, by luck. We do not step into it by some mysterious providence guiding our feet in spite of our rebelliousness, carelessness, neglect, or indifference. We shall not walk at last through the gates of the city beyond the stars because we happened to drift at random into the company of those who shall walk there. Blind chance has absolutely no part to play in salvation.[1]

On the contrary, those who walk in triumph through heaven's wide-swinging gates will do so because they will have gained the victory over the world, the flesh, and the devil. And to do so will take everything they have.

> No one will be *carried* borne upward without *severe study* stern, persevering effort in his own behalf. All must engage in this warfare for themselves. Individually we are responsible for the issue of the struggle; though Noah, Job, and Daniel were in the land, they could deliver neither son nor daughter by their righteousness.—*Testimonies*, vol. 8, pp. 313, 314.
>
> We have great victories to gain, and a heaven to lose if we do not gain them.—*Ibid.*, vol. 5, p. 267.

In pondering my approach to this book I recognized a problem—indeed, a danger—inherent in writing a manuscript of this nature: the problem of balance and the danger involved in imbalance.

A certain emphasis will be found in this book because of the very nature of my subject. This emphasis could lead to misunderstanding on the part of some. The apostle James, in his accentuation of works in his theme of working faith, caused Martin Luther to *criticize, put down* belittle his letter as "an epistle of straw." Others have had similar problems with James. And there are those who have problems with other parts of the

---

[1] See Appendix (p. 157) for Spirit of Prophecy statements indicated by superior figures.

14

Holy Scriptures for similar reasons.

Moreover, I remember Ellen White's caution to "Brother K," as found in *Selected Messages*, book 1, pages 176, 177. Her admonitions there regarding the expressing of ideas in such a way as to be misunderstood and to cause problems must be taken very seriously.

In writing, I recalled words by Konrad Adenauer, former Chancellor of West Germany: "We are all under the same sky, but we don't all have the same horizon."

This book is written from the particular point where I see the horizon. It is penned as growing from my study, my observations, my experience. In doing this, I have tried to keep my eyes as much as possible away from the horizon, and toward the sky that covers us all. I have also tried to look beyond the sky we see, to Him who knows and respects us all as individuals, remembering at the same time that His conditions and standards are immovable, eternal.

The Terminal Cancer of Sin

Having said this, let me add to this chapter this thought: Early in his final book, *Stay of Execution,* the late eminent journalist Stewart Alsop tells of being a patient at the National Institutes of Health, Bethesda, Maryland, suffering from leukemia. Wandering around one day on his floor, he entered a staff room where he saw a sign not meant to be seen by patients: ALL PATIENTS MUST HAVE INCURABLE CANCER. ALL PATIENTS MUST BE FRANKLY INFORMED OF THEIR CASE.

Reading the sign, Mr. Alsop felt "a dark pit of fear" inside.

Stewart Alsop died of cancer.

Can we face this fact for a moment? We are all suffering from the terminal cancer of sin. We are all sinners, and "the soul that sinneth, it shall die."

We can be treated with soft, reassuring, don't-get-excited, don't-be-concerned words—and die in our sins. Or we can be told, without deception, clearly, what our problem is.[2]

In physical cancer it will be recognized that the physician may tell his patient ever so gently and compassionately of his disease. But the news is still going to be traumatic. But in spiritual cancer we can be told of the tremendous remedy that is found in the Lord Jesus, and how that remedy works 100 per cent for us if we will faithfully place ourselves into the hands of the Great Physician.

So I decided to describe plainly, depending upon the Bible and the Spirit of Prophecy, what seems to be the difficulty of many of us who are church members. I do this so that, like the patients in the cancer ward of the National Institutes of Health, we might understand the gravity of our situation. When we do this it is possible for us to see the importance of availing ourselves of the glorious remedy provided.

In a book of this nature, besides the problems already referred to, there is the problem of what to include. Some readers may feel I have written too much on one phase of my subject; others, that I have written too little. Some may think I have left out material that should be included; others, that I have included matter that should be left out. In any case, I have written from my own perspective with the objective, hopefully, of helping some reader find a meaningful, victorious relationship with Jesus.

In Brief

Victory connotes struggle. The word has no meaning apart from struggle. So this book is about the Christian's struggle that leads to final victory.

The Christian warfare is not lightly, and must not be ignorantly, entered into. "What king," asked Jesus, "going to encounter another king in war, will not sit down first and take counsel?" (Luke 14:31, R.S.V.).

In this book we shall be taking a candid look at our assets and liabilities, with liabilities examined first. They may look large and discouraging. We shall also consider what is required of us before we can really begin to gain victories. We may consider this rather big, also.

Then we shall consider our allies, and shall discover that with them we cannot possibly lose the war.

Following this, looking at methods and means by which victory is gained, we shall discover great demands, but

greater possibilities, and still greater potential conquests
that climax in the glorious and triumphant event described
by the revelator:

> And after this I beheld, and, lo, a great multitude, which no man
> could number, of all nations, and kindreds, and people, and tongues
> stood before the throne, and before the Lamb, clothed with white
> robes, and palms in their hands; and cried with a loud voice, saying,
> Salvation to our God which sitteth upon the throne, and unto the
> Lamb. . . . And one of the elders answered, saying unto me, What
> are these which are arrayed in white robes? and whence came they?
> And I said unto him, Sir, thou knowest. And he said to me, These
> are they which came out of great tribulation, and have washed their
> robes, and made them white in the blood of the Lamb. Therefore
> are they before the throne of God, and serve him day and night in
> his temple: and he that sitteth on the throne shall dwell among
> them. They shall hunger no more, neither thirst any more; neither
> shall the sun light on them, nor any heat. For the Lamb which is in
> the midst of the throne shall feed them, and shall lead them unto
> living fountains of waters: and God shall wipe away all tears from
> their eyes (Rev. 7:9-17).

Willard Saxby and the Laodiceans

ACCORDING to the Seventh-day Adventist *Yearbooks* for 1890 to 1894, Willard H. Saxby, an ordained minister of the Seventh-day Adventist Church, served in Ohio during those years. He may have ministered there as late as 1902 or 1903. During those years no *Yearbooks* were published. Consequently, we cannot be sure when he moved from Ohio to Washington State, where his address is listed in the 1904 *Yearbook*.

Sometime during the five or six or more years Elder Saxby worked in Ohio, Ellen White wrote a letter that told him some things about himself he had trouble seeing and accepting.

Elder Saxby received the testimony during a camp meeting he was attending in Ohio. It was part of a letter dealing with other matters, sent in care of a leading brother. The testimony for Elder Saxby was delivered to him following the close of one of the evening meetings.

While the other minister, whom Elder Saxby refers to as Elder A, and he sat together in the latter's tent, Elder A asked Elder Saxby whether he believed in the *Testimonies*. To this question Saxby answered decidedly in the affirmative. Then, after they had prayed together, Elder A slowly read the letter, which was in Mrs. White's handwriting.

The manuscript was eleven pages long. The first five

were for Elder Saxby personally.

After Elder A had read a few paragraphs he came to a statement to which Saxby strongly objected. "That is not so!" he exclaimed, emphatically.

"Brother Saxby, you say it is so, and the Lord will help you to see that it is so."

"But how can I say a thing is so when I know it is not so?" Elder Saxby protested.

"Brother Saxby, you say it is so, and the Lord will help you to see that it is so," Elder A repeated. With that he continued reading.

A page or so farther along Elder A read another statement to which Willard Saxby objected, "That is not so!"

Again Elder A answered the protestation by saying substantially what he had said before. Then, after making a few other observations, he began to read the letter again.

There were four personal statements in the letter to which Willard Saxby took exception. On the first he was especially positive.

The letter finished, Elder Saxby received permission to take it home and return it the next day.

When he got to his room Willard Saxby found his wife in bed, but awake, anxiously wondering what had detained him. When he told her his experience she asked him to read the testimony from Sister White. He demurred, saying it was too late to read it all. But he agreed to share with her the one paragraph with which he had his greatest problem. Before he read it he told his wife that he had insisted to Elder A that what Sister White had written was not so.

The statement in question had to do with a matter between Saxby and his wife. After he had read it, Mrs. Saxby abruptly sat up in bed and, emphatically pointing her finger at him, said with all the earnestness of which she was capable, *"Willard, that is so!"*

Three Against One

Describing his reaction to his wife's exclamation, Elder Saxby wrote:

I began to reason very seriously, like this: My wife says it is so;

and Elder A, because of his confidence in the Spirit of Prophecy, says it is so; and, above all, the Lord through His servant says it is so: it must be so—three against one. As I sought the Lord by fasting and prayer, I soon saw things in the true light. The testimony was a photograph of my inner life, and I could see that it was.—*Review and Herald,* May 18, 1916.

Let us leave Willard Saxby for a little and consider another matter.

Picture a man walking down a street naked, blindly groping around, not knowing where he is or where he is going—a most pitiable wretch indeed.

But when he is approached by a concerned would-be benefactor, he says, "I am rich! I am doing very well. I have everything I want."

We would hardly know what to make of such a person.

But suppose that, instead of one man, there were a hundred, a thousand, a million in that miserable condition, all protesting, "I am rich. I have prospered. There is nothing I need."

The idea is, of course, too preposterous to think about seriously. How could a single normal person, to say nothing of scores, or thousands, or more, be wretched and not know it? How could he be miserable and totally unaware of it? Poor, and think himself prosperous? Blind and naked, fancying that he could see and that he was clothed?

We say again, the idea is too preposterous to consider seriously.

Or is it?

We hesitate to make an application, but Inspiration does it for us.

To the angel of the church in Laodicea write: . . . You say, I am rich, I have prospered, and I need nothing; not knowing that you are wretched, pitiable, poor, blind, and naked" (Rev. 3:14-17, R.S.V.).

The Laodicean message applies to the people of God who profess to believe present truth. The greater part are lukewarm professors, having a name but no zeal.—*Testimonies,* vol. 4, p. 87.

The message to the Laodiceans is applicable to Seventh-day Adventists who have had great light and have not walked in the light. It is those who have made great profession, but have not kept in step with their Leader, that will be spewed out of His mouth unless they repent.—*Selected Messages*, book 2, p. 66.

Diagrammatically, then, the Laodicean message may be depicted like this:

COLD
Worldly

LUKEWARM
"The greater part are lukewarm professors"

HOT
Committed
few

As with other passages of the Bible and the Spirit of Prophecy we have examined, the implications of this picture are solemn. For we read, "Because thou art lukewarm . . . I will spue thee out of my mouth" (Rev. 3:16). Says *The SDA Bible Commentary* on the text: "The figure of tepid water is pressed to its logical conclusion. Such water is disappointing and nauseating, and the one who drinks it almost involuntarily expels it."

I must ask myself, In which of the three groups am I? The cold, lukewarm, or hot? [3]

"What Greater Deception?"

What greater deception can come upon human minds than a confidence that they are right when they are all wrong! The message of the True Witness finds the people of God in a sad deception, yet honest in that deception. They know not that their condition is deplorable in the sight of God. While those addressed are flattering themselves that they are in an exalted spiritual condition, the message of the True Witness breaks their security by the startling denunciation of their true condition of spiritual blindness, poverty, and wretchedness. The testimony, so cutting and severe, cannot be a mistake, for it is the True Witness who speaks, and His testimony must be correct.—*Testimonies*, vol. 3, pp. 252, 253.

The Ellen G. White Comments in the message to the Laodicean church in volume seven of *The Seventh-day Adventist Bible Commentary* comprise some eight pages (pp. 959-967). In these pages are found more than a score of words and phrases that she used to describe the Laodicean

21

condition. Other descriptions may be found in other places in her writings.

Each individual church member is called upon to examine frankly and prayerfully his own religious experience in the light of these descriptions. Among them are: "selfishness"; "destitute of . . . meekness"; a "tame, lifeless, emotionless religious experience"; "halfhearted Christians"; "self-sufficiency"; "spiritual self-deception"; the taking of a "noncommittal position" in spiritual things; lacking lowliness; satisfied in their own "self-security"; "selfish egotism"; "self-exaltation"; "hypocrisy"; "self-love"; "vain conceit"; "willfully ignorant"; "indulgence of pride"; "covetousness"; "worldly ambition."

These are stark, flinty, brutally frank observations. "The testimony of the True Witness is not a smooth message."— *Testimonies,* vol. 3, p. 257. It is a "fearful message" (*ibid.,* vol. 1, p. 186). We rebel at making personal applications. Our instinct is to turn from them and to think of more pleasant things, or to decide they do not apply to us.

But dare we so quickly push them aside? Only, perhaps, at the peril of our souls.

Let us turn to another message brought to the church of the last days by the Lord.

In Matthew 25:1-13 is recorded Christ's parable of the ten virgins, which virgins represent those who await His return.

Invited to a wedding, which in the East frequently was held at night, the ten maidens took their lamps with them. But five neglected to take sufficient oil. The hour began to grow late; yet the bridegroom had not come, so all ten went to sleep.

Then, at midnight, a shout went up, "Look, the bridegroom is coming. Go out to meet him."

Startled, the ten awoke and looked at their lamps. Then the foolish maidens were dismayed to discover that their lamps were going out, and they had no oil in their flasks. An appeal to the other five for oil brought refusal—they had only enough for themselves.

Greatly worried, the five hastened to find oil. But, when

they returned to the house where the marriage was being held, they found the door closed and locked. Their urgent call to be let in only brought the chilling response from the bridegroom, "I tell you, I do not know you."

pay attention to

This parable applies to the Laodiceans who do not heed the warnings and invitations that come to them to secure the oil, which is "the righteousness of Christ. It represents character, and character is not transferable."—*Testimonies to Ministers*, p. 234.

attempt

Finally they awake and endeavor to correct their mistake, to remodel their characters. But, unutterably sadly, it is too late! Probation has closed.[4]

without words

Not Hypocrites

But notice:

Someone that pretends to be good / virtue

moral excellence

The class represented by the foolish virgins are not hypocrites. They have a regard for the truth, they have advocated the truth, they are attracted to those who believe the truth; but they have not yielded themselves to the Holy Spirit's working. They have not fallen upon the Rock Christ Jesus, and permitted their old nature to be broken up.—*Christ's Object Lessons*, p. 411.

submitted

Continuing, Ellen White says:

The class represented by the foolish virgins have been content with a superficial work. They do not know God. They have not studied His character; they have not held communion with Him; therefore they do not know how to trust, how to look and live.—*Ibid.*

The condition of the Laodiceans and the ten virgins is essentially the same, except that the parable describes their condition when probation closes.

The Laodiceans are not "cold," meaning they are not totally rebellious. It is not that they never made a profession of Christianity; they are just not "hot," not fully given over to God. They are "lukewarm," uncommitted, unsurrendered to God. "The message of the True Witness finds the people of God [the Laodiceans] in a sad deception, yet honest in that deception."—*Testimonies*, vol. 3, p. 253. The parallel description of the ten virgins is that they are not hypocrites, but have been content with a superficial work. Like the

23

Laodiceans, they are in an uncommitted, unsurrendered condition.

Willard Saxby was at first positive that the message from Ellen White did not apply to him, that she was mistaken. But the realization that she, his wife, and Elder A all felt that it did, caused him soberly and seriously to examine himself. As a result of his consequent examination of his heart and life, he was led to the conclusion that the message did indeed apply to himself.

We, the Seventh-day Adventist people today, may be tempted to feel that the Laodicean message in its interpretation and application in the Spirit of Prophecy writings does not apply to us, *personally.* To Brother Jones and Sister Smith, possibly. But to me! [5]

Ellen White stated that the message applies to "the greater part" of the church. Note: The message is recorded in Scriptures for the last church, for us who are living today. The messenger to the remnant church states that it applies to us. Does my conscience, and does yours, suggest that perhaps the message does apply to us, personally? Three to one?

"Examine yourselves: are you living the life of faith? Put yourselves to the test" (2 Cor. 13:5, N.E.B.).*

> Determine to know the worst of your case. Ascertain if you have an inheritance on high. Deal truly with your own soul.—*Testimonies,* vol. 1, p. 163.
> With fasting and earnest prayer, with deep heart searching, stern self-examination, lay bare the soul; let no act escape your critical examination.—*Ibid.,* vol. 2, p. 158.
> Those who have no time to give attention to their own souls, to examine themselves daily whether they be in the love of God, and place themselves in the channel of light, will have time to give to the suggestions of Satan and the working out of his plans.—*Selected Messages,* book 2, pp. 20, 21.

Not a Hopeless Case

The Laodicean message is not a hopeless case but a most sobering one.

---

* Texts credited to N.E.B. are from *The New English Bible.* © The Delegates of the Oxford University Press and the Syndics of the Cambridge University Press 1970. Reprinted by permission.

fall back in bad behaviour.

Willard Saxby and the Laodiceans

But the counsel of the True Witness does not represent those who are lukewarm as in a hopeless case. There is yet a chance to remedy their state, and the Laodicean message is full of encouragement; for the backslidden church may yet buy the gold of faith and love, may yet have the white robe of the righteousness of Christ, that the shame of their nakedness need not appear. Purity of heart, purity of motive, may yet characterize those who are half-hearted and who are striving to serve God and Mammon. *material possessions* They may yet wash their robes of character and make them white in the blood of the Lamb.—*Review and Herald,* Aug. 28, 1894.

The True Witness faithfully diagnoses the case and prescribes the remedy: the white raiment, the righteousness of Christ wrought out *formed out* in the character; gold, faith in God; and eyesalve, *soothing influence* which is God's Word. This "salve" "makes the conscience smart under its application; for it *feeling distressed* convicts of sin. But the smarting is necessary that the healing may follow, and the eye be single to the glory of God."—*The SDA Bible Commentary,* Ellen G. White Comments, on Rev. 3:18, p. 965.

Each of these gifts—the gold, the eyesalve, and the white raiment—comes through the grace of God. "It is through the impartation *conveying* of the grace of Christ that sin is discerned in its hateful nature, and finally driven from the soul temple."—*Review and Herald,* Nov. 4, 1890.

The Laodicean message is a frank, *direct* unflattering, *with sincerity* soul-searching message. But it is one we need to be glad God brings to us. For without it we would continue in our spiritual lethargy until it was too late.

As many as I love, I rebuke *indifference* *reprove* and chasten: be zealous *discipline* *eager* therefore, and repent. Behold, I stand at the door, and knock: if any man hear my voice, and open the door, I will come in to him, and will sup with him, and he with me. To him that overcometh will I grant to sit with me in my throne, even as I also overcame, and am set down with my Father in his throne. He that hath an ear, let him hear what the Spirit saith unto the churches (Rev. 3:19-22).

Can we go on being unresponsive to Jesus' love? Can we permit Him to stand waiting outside our lives, patiently seeking an invitation to come in? Shall we not open our hearts and minds and allow Him earnestly *seriously* and candidly, *straightforward* but compassionately, *mercifully* to unfold to us our needs? Shall we not accept from Him the only remedy that is available for our spiritual ills?

If we do not, we shall be cheating ourselves of forgiveness, the removal of the sense of guilt, of peace, of eternity. What rational being could choose such loss?

The Irreducible Minimum

LOVE is the dominant characteristic of God, and love is outgoing. God's love reaches out to bestow its warmth upon the whole of His creation.

But love desires response, and God yearns *desires* for a willing return of His love from all His creatures. Sadly, He has not received that response from many of mankind for six thousand years, for our race has been in rebellion against its Creator.

During all that time God has been trying to bring humanity back into the warm circle of His love. But He has been able to do so for only a very few, relatively. Many have not been interested. And some who have been interested have never entered into the circle, because they were not willing to meet the conditions God had to require.

He has made His requirements as few and easy as possible. But requirements there must be. For to accept those who would not accept them would mean that sin, which must be excluded at all costs (Christ gave His all that sin might be excluded, and yet mankind be saved), would be preserved and contaminate heaven. That cannot be!

So God says to you and me, "I want, above anything else, to have you in My kingdom. I gave My Son that you might be there. But the very stability, the preservation, of My kingdom demands that I make certain minimum requirements. This is the way it has to be. Please meet those requirements! I want you to be with Me!"

The irreducible minimum that God must require is expressed in the words of Jesus to the Pharisee, Nicodemus: "Jesus . . . said unto him, Verily, verily, I say unto thee, Except a man be born again, he cannot see the kingdom of God" (John 3:3).

Plain Words

These words are as unequivocal, as straightforward, as it is possible for words to be. Uttered as they were in love, nevertheless they made it plain that there is no possibility of receiving eternal life, of having a part in the heavenly kingdom to come, except as one experiences what is termed the new birth.

The words of Jesus are so plain that there is but one major question one needs to ask in order that he may fully understand what they mean: What is this experience of the new birth without which no man shall see heaven?

The Bible makes it vividly clear that the new birth means a radical change in the life: "Therefore if any man be in Christ, he is a new creature: old things are passed away; behold, all things are become new" (2 Cor. 5:17); "A new heart also will I give you, and a new spirit will I put within you; and I will take away the stony heart out of your flesh, and I will give you an heart of flesh" (Eze. 36:26).

The fact that the newborn person is described as "a new creature," or creation, for which "all things have become new," who has "set . . . [his] feet upon the new path of life" (Rom. 6:4, N.E.B.), clearly indicates a fundamental, basic change. It is not a grafting of new shoots into the old tree. It is a new and different kind of tree.

Not a Modified or Rearranged Life

It is not a modified life in which the sinner stops drinking and smoking, in which he tries a bit harder to control his temper, appetite, and entertainment habits. It is not merely an altered life, in which jewelry is left off, in which one day in seven is now spent differently from before, in which newly adopted beliefs cause him to change friends and the use of time.[6]

It is not merely a rearranged life in which he shifts priorities; in which, for example, he moves sports or money, jobs or dress, entertainment or eating, and so on, from a high place of priority to a lower place.[7]

> The Christian's life is not a modification or improvement of the old, but a transformation of nature. There is a death to self and sin, and a new life altogether. This change can be brought about only by the effectual working of the Holy Spirit.—*The Desire of Ages,* p. 172.

It is an experience that all, without exception, must have who are to be recognized as members of the family of God. There are none who came into the world born again, who might be referred to as natural Christians and therefore not needing the experience.

> A natural Christian! This deceptive idea has served many as a garment of self-righteousness, and has led many to a supposed hope in Christ, who had no experimental knowledge of Him, of His experience, His trials, His life of self-denial and self-sacrifice.— *Testimonies,* vol. 2, pp. 177, 178.
> Your birth, your reputation, your wealth, your talents, your virtues, your piety, your philanthropy, or anything else in you or connected with you, will not form a bond of union between your soul and Christ.—*Ibid.,* vol. 5, pp. 48, 49.

In the new-birth transformation, life meets

> a change so marked as to be represented by death. From living, active life, to death! What a striking figure! None need be deceived here. If this transformation has not been experienced by you, rest not. Seek the Lord with all your hearts. Make this the all-important business of your lives.—*Ibid.,* vol. 2, p. 179.[8]

"Rest not" till you have received this transformed nature, Mrs. White exhorted. We may remember that God, in unsleeping love, is active to bring every person to Himself.

What are the signs by which we may know whether we are born again? The Bible supplies many. For example, the Beatitudes (Matt. 5:3-12) relate to men and women who have had the experience. Galatians 5 contrasts the evil works and attitudes of the unregenerate (verses 19-21), with the fruit of the Spirit as seen in the regenerate (verses 22, 23).

29

Nine Signs of Regeneration

I suggest nine manifestations of the new-birth experience:

(1) **A sense of freedom: peace in the soul.** The individual, especially the professed Christian who is not truly born again, who is still wrestling with unwanted sins and is haunted by guilt, cannot have peace. Beset by doubts, uncertain as to his status with God, he is often sad.

But with the new-birth experience, all that is changed. "Therefore being justified by faith [and thus pardoned], we have peace with God through our Lord Jesus Christ" (Rom. 5:1). Ellen White describes the experience beautifully by saying in *The Ministry of Healing*, page 58, "There is silence in the soul." All the tumult, all the strife is over because Jesus reigns completely, sin is expelled, and self no longer reigns.[9]

> He who is at peace with God and his fellow-men cannot be made miserable. Envy will not be in his heart; evil surmisings will find no room there; hatred cannot exist. The heart that is in harmony with God is a partaker of the peace of heaven, and will diffuse its blessed influence on all around.—*Thoughts From the Mount of Blessing*, p. 28.[10]

(2) **An experience of love for others.** "We know that we have passed out of death into life, because we love the brethren. He who does not love abides in death" (1 John 3:14, N.A.S.B.). This Christian love is not sentimental feeling, or even necessarily that emotion found among members of a family. It is an attitude of regard, a reasoned concern for the interests of others, a deliberate decision to further others' welfare as needed.

This attitude is maintained for the unintelligent, the eccentric, the unlovable, the down-and-outer, for an enemy, as well as for a friend. It is a principle that prompts one, in attitude and action, to put the welfare of others before his own.[11]

It is this love that we need to possess. Without it all other virtues and gifts are as nothing (cf. 1 Cor. 13). It is of this love that John says, "He that loveth not knoweth not God; for God is love" (1 John 4:8). This love can come only from

30

God; no man can generate such a broad spectrum of love of himself. It is not a deepening or refining of human love. It is a divine gift. It is greater even than the love of a mother for her child (see *Messages to Young People,* p. 115). "[Pure] love is a heavenly attribute. The natural heart cannot originate it. This heavenly plant only flourishes where Christ reigns supreme."—*The SDA Bible Commentary,* Ellen G. White Comments, on 1 John 4:7, 8, p. 952.

(3) **A turning of mind and heart from the world.** The un- *not renewed* regenerate person is naturally of the world. His main interests are normally centered there, and cannot be expected to be otherwise. He is job-centered, or money-centered, entertainment-centered,[12] position-centered, or clothes-centered, may be even work-for-the-Lord centered.[13]

The born-again person will not remain in embarrassed silence when the conversation is about Jesus and His love, yet talk enthusiastically about sports, clothes, travel, or cars.[14]

Those who give themselves to Christ "are not of this world" (John 17:14).[15]

practical Real conversion is a decided change of feelings and motives; it *hurrying* is a virtual taking leave of worldly connections, a hastening from their spiritual atmosphere, a withdrawing from the controlling power of their thoughts, opinions, and influences.—*Testimonies,* vol. 5, pp. 82, 83.

(4) **Victory where before was defeat.** The person seeking to overcome in his own strength, or mainly in his own strength, cannot be victorious. The reason is that it is a case of self trying to cast out self, which is impossible.

The person who does not have Jesus dwelling within cannot be victorious. Thus, only the born-again person can have sustained victories over his sins. Only the person who can apply to himself Paul's words, "I live; yet not I, but Christ liveth in me," can overcome sin. He can then say, "I can do all things through Christ which strengtheneth me."[16]

This does not by any means suggest that there will not be terrible struggles in the Christian's life sometimes. The mortification of self is a daily, even momentary, work. But because the mind is now changed, and the desires, inclina-

controlling

tions, motives, and will of the born-again person is Christ-directed, he can gain the victory.

> If you are "willing to be made willing," God will accomplish the work for you, even "casting down imaginations, and every high thing that exalteth itself against the knowledge of God, and bringing into captivity every thought to the obedience of Christ." Then you will work out your own salvation with fear and trembling. "For it is God which worketh in you, both to will and to do of His good pleasure."—*Thoughts From the Mount of Blessing*, pp. 142, 143.

⑤ **A frequent, instinctive inclination to pray.** This desire comes as a deep-down yearning to commune with the Saviour, as the lover has a strong desire to be with the person who is the object of his affections. This urge is poetically expressed by the psalmist: "As the hart panteth after the water brooks, so panteth my soul after thee, O God. My soul thirsteth for God, for the living God" (Ps. 42:1, 2).

⑥ **An interest in and turning to God's Word.** "Thy words were found, and I did eat them; and thy word was unto me the joy and rejoicing of mine heart," wrote Jeremiah (Jer. 15:16).[17] To the born-again person—

> the word of God, which was dull and uninteresting, is now chosen as his study, the man of his counsel. It is as a letter written to him from God, bearing the inscription of the Eternal. His thoughts, his words, and his deeds are brought to this rule and tested. He trembles at the commands and threatenings which it contains, while he firmly grasps its promises and strengthens his soul by appropriating them to himself.—*The Faith I Live By*, p. 139.

⑦ **A growing sensitivity to sin.** "While we were spiritually dead in our disobedience he [God] brought us to life with Christ" (Eph. 2:5, T.E.V.).[18] In commenting on Paul's words here, Ellen White, writing of the new birth, says:

> New thoughts, new feelings, new motives, are implanted. A new standard of character is set up—the life of Christ. The mind is changed; the faculties are roused to action in new lines. . . . The conscience is awakened.—*Christ's Object Lessons*, pp. 98, 99.
>
> When the heart yields to the influence of the Spirit of God, the conscience will be quickened.—*Steps to Christ*, p. 24.

As many can testify, the question "What's wrong with it?" is often solved for the questioner when the Holy Spirit is able to awaken the slumbering conscience and help us see what is indeed wrong with it."

It is like a beam of sunlight shining through a tiny hole in a closed blind into a darkened room. In the beam are seen hundreds of dust motes floating in the air that were not seen before. So it is that when the Sun of Righteousness shines in our lives we see sins we were not aware of before.

An attitude of willing obedience to God. The exclamation "I delight to do thy will, O my God" (Ps. 40:8) can be the words of the born-again person only (cf. Jer. 31:33). The unregenerate heart "is not subject to the law of God, neither indeed can be" (Rom. 8:7).

> In the new birth the heart is brought into harmony with God, as it is brought into accord with His law. When this mighty change has taken place in the sinner, he has passed from death unto life, from sin unto holiness, from transgression and rebellion to obedience and loyalty. The old life of alienation from God has ended; the new life of reconciliation, of faith and love, has begun.—*The Great Controversy*, p. 468.
>
> Whenever one renounces sin, which is the transgression of the law, his life will be brought into conformity to the law, into perfect obedience. This is the work of the Holy Spirit. . . . Love is manifested in obedience. The line of demarcation will be plain and distinct between those who love God and keep His commandments, and those who love Him not and disregard His precepts.—*Testimonies*, vol. 6, p. 92.

This attitude of obedience will be not only toward those requirements that are easy and convenient but also toward those that demand self-denial and self-sacrifice."

An impulse to witness to others. Jesus' final words to His disciples was the promise of the Holy Spirit. When He should be received, then, said Jesus, "you shall be my witnesses" (Acts 1:8, R.S.V.). David, in beseeching God for forgiveness and restoration to His favor—to the "joy of thy salvation"—continued, "Then I will teach transgressors thy ways, and sinners will return to thee" (Ps. 51:12, 13, R.S.V.).

> If we are Christians, this work [witnessing] will be our delight. No sooner is one converted than there is born within him a desire to make known to others what a precious friend he has found in Jesus. The saving and sanctifying truth cannot be shut up in his heart.—*The Desire of Ages*, p. 141.

3

Just as soon as a person is really converted to the truth there springs up in his heart an earnest desire to go and tell some friends or neighbor of the precious light shining forth from the sacred pages. In his unselfish labor to save others he is a living epistle, known and read of all men. His life shows that he has been converted to Christ and has become a colaborer with Him.—*Testimonies*, vol. 5, p. 386.

In his deeply spiritual book, *God's Way of Holiness*, Horatius Bonar begins one chapter thus:

Before I can live a Christian life, I must be a Christian man. Am I such? I ought to *know* this. Do I know it, and, in knowing it, know whose I am, and whom I serve? Or is my title to the name still questionable, still a matter of anxious debate and search?

If I am to *live* as a son of God, I must *be* a son, and I must *know* it; otherwise my life will be an artificial imitation, a piece of barren mechanism, performing certain excellent movements, but destitute of vital heat and force. Here many fail. They try to *live* like sons, in order to *make* themselves sons, forgetting God's simple plan for attaining sonship at once, "As many as received him, to them gave he power to become the sons of God" (John 1:12).—Page 57.

Sons and daughters have certain characteristics of their fathers. Do I have the characteristics of my heavenly Father?

The One Who Helps Us Cope

CENTRAL to the matters discussed in this book, which, in a nutshell, are the new birth, justification, and sanctification, is the operation of the Holy Spirit. The fulfilling of the plan of salvation, which makes those transactions possible in and for man, depends upon the Holy Spirit's ministry.

There are few passages in Scripture that so clearly and dramatically highlight the work of the Spirit in man's salvation as Romans 7 and 8. In chapter seven Paul, with distinct brush strokes, draws for us a picture of his own experience when he eventually saw the claims of God and His law upon him:

> We know that the law is spiritual; but I am carnal, sold under sin. I do not understand my own actions. For I do not do what I want, but I do the very thing I hate. Now if I do what I do not want, I agree that the law is good. So then it is no longer I that do it, but sin which dwells within me. For I know that nothing good dwells within me, that is, in my flesh. I can will what is right, but I cannot do it. For I do not do the good I want, but the evil I do not want is what I do. Now if I do what I do not want, it is no longer I that do it, but sin which dwells within me (Rom. 7:14-20, R.S.V.).

Then he observes—

> I delight in the law of God, in my inmost self, but I see in my members another law at war with the law of my mind and making me captive to the law of sin which dwells in my members (verses 22, 23, R.S.V.).

Three Laws

In these words Paul sets forth two laws. The principle of God's law, epitomized by the Ten Commandments (cf. verse 7), the claims of which he acknowledges as fair and good, but which he could not meet, and "the law of sin which dwells in my members." This law may be defined, briefly, as those inherited and cultivated tendencies to sin that make it humanly impossible to do right unaided; those limitations and weaknesses that are a part of man's mortality. Thus, frustrated by the impedances of his human nature and in a state of great inner tension because of them, Paul cries out desperately, "Wretched man that I am! Who will deliver me from this body of death?" (verse 24, R.S.V.).

But in Romans 8 we have the tension resolved, for a *third law* enters that totally relieves the spiritual strain and solves Paul's entire problem: "For the law of the Spirit of life in Christ Jesus has set me free from the law of sin and death" (chap. 8:2, R.S.V.).[n]

What may we understand this third law, or better, principle, to be? It may be defined as the manner in which the Holy Spirit works when He comes into the surrendered life.

So Paul makes it unmistakably plain that the Holy Spirit, and only the Holy Spirit as Christ's representative, can do for man what must be done for him if he is to gain the victory over his sins, have peace and joy within, and gain eternal life.

We understand, then, that the efficacy even of the work of Christ Himself for man is dependent upon the Holy Spirit. Without Him, everything that was done by Jesus during His earthly life—in Gethsemane, upon the cross, in arising from the tomb—and in His priestly ministry in heaven, would be unfruitful. The benefits of that which Christ did would be of little more usefulness than any of the world's great religious or ethical leaders. For even though He was God, and they were only men, Christ could not change men merely by His example and teachings. To change them it was necessary to work within them. And this work is done by the Holy Spirit, the Spirit of Christ, who was sent to do in men's hearts the work Jesus had made possible.

> The Holy Spirit was the highest of all gifts that He [Christ] could solicit from His Father for the exaltation of His people. The Spirit was to be given as a regenerating agent, *and without this the sacrifice of Christ would have been of no avail.* . . . It is the Spirit that makes effectual what has been wrought out by the world's Redeemer. It is by the Spirit that the heart is made pure. Through the Spirit the believer becomes a partaker of the divine nature. Christ has given His Spirit as a divine power to overcome all hereditary and cultivated tendencies to evil, and to impress His own character upon His church.—*The Desire of Ages,* p. 671. (Italics supplied.)

The Greatest Gift Promised

Jesus promised His disciples the gift of the Spirit during His last hours with them before going to Gethsemane, the halls of Caiaphas, Herod, and Pilate—and to Calvary. For three years He had taught them by word and example. For three years He had been their strength, counselor, guide, helper, and friend. Now He was to leave them as sheep among wolves, as doves among serpents.

Knowing their great need better than they ever could, and what the future held for them, He sought the best gift He could bestow that would meet their many needs.

"I will pray the Father," He said, "and he shall give you another Comforter, that he may abide with you for ever; even the Spirit of truth" (John 14:16, 17).

The Greek term translated Comforter in the King James Version is *paraklētos.* It is variously rendered in other versions as "Helper" (Moffatt, N.A.S.B.), "Counselor" (R.S.V.), "Advocate" (N.E.B.), "someone else to stand by you" (Phillips), and by other terms in other versions. The variety of translations suggests that the word has a rich possibility of meanings. This is true.

The popular Scottish author and theologian William Barclay has an interesting passage in one of his books in which he explains the breadth of meaning of the word *paraklētos:*

> The word *paraklētos* really means *someone who is called in;* but it is the reason *why* the person is called in which gives the word

37

its distinctive associations. The Greeks used the word in a wide variety of ways. A *paraklētos* might be a person *called in* to give witness in a law court in someone's favor; he might be an advocate *called in* to plead someone's cause when someone was under a charge which would issue in serious penalty; he might be an expert *called in* to give advice in some difficult situation. He might be a person *called in* when, for example, a company of soldiers were depressed and dispirited to put new courage into their minds and hearts. Always a *paraklētos* is *someone called in to help* when the person who calls him in is in trouble or distress or doubt or bewilderment. . . . We have a modern phrase which we often use. We talk of being able *to cope* with things. That is precisely the work of the Holy Spirit. The Holy Spirit comes to us and takes away our inadequacies and enables us to cope with life. The Holy Spirit substitutes victorious for defeated living.—*The Gospel of John,* vol. 2, pp. 194, 195.

The Fellowship of the Spirit

Paul uses a word that conveys something of the same idea as *paraklētos,* adding perhaps a further dimension. He writes of the "fellowship" of the Spirit (Phil. 2:1; 2 Cor. 13:14, R.S.V.). The Greek term *koinōnia* suggests an intimate communion and sympathetic cooperation of the third member of the Godhead with the Christian.

> At all times and in all places, in all sorrows and in all afflictions, when the outlook seems dark and the future perplexing, and we feel helpless and alone, the Comforter will be sent in answer to the prayer of faith. Circumstances may separate us from every earthly friend; but no circumstance, no distance, can separate us from the heavenly Comforter. Wherever we are, wherever we may go, He is always at our right hand to support, sustain, uphold, and cheer.—*The Desire of Ages,* pp. 669, 670.

Explaining to His disciples the value of the Gift He was sending, Jesus told them that the Holy Spirit would convict men of their sins; persuade them of the truth of the gospel, and of the greatness of Christ's righteousness; and assure them that it might be theirs (John 16:8-10). Thus the Holy Spirit is the active agent in conversion (chap. 3:5; Titus 3:5, 6). If men refused or neglected to separate from their sins and accept Jesus' righteousness the Spirit would press upon them a consciousness of the frightening results of what they were doing (John 16:11).

Also, by the Holy Spirit, we are cleansed, set apart as God's children, and justified (1 Cor. 6:11, N.E.B.). By the Spirit the warfare in the heart and life is successfully carried on, and the Christian fruits are developed (Gal. 5:16-25). Further, the work of the Holy Spirit is to develop righteousness, and to give peace and joy (Rom. 14:17), to guide into truth (John 14:13), to help in weakness (Rom. 8:26, R.S.V.), to provide strength (Eph. 3:16) and power (Luke 24:49), to free from sin (2 Cor. 3:17), and to keep us from sinning.

As we understand what the Holy Spirit does for us, we can appreciate the statement that when His power comes into our lives it brings "all other blessings in its train" (*The Acts of the Apostles,* p. 50). We greatly need those blessings. We need the help of the Spirit to cope with sin and self, and to expel them from our lives. Therefore, before we continue to read the pages of this book, shall we not follow the counsel of the Spirit of Prophecy and "seek the aid of God's Spirit by prayer" (*Testimonies to Ministers,* p. 456)? [22]

The Heart of the Matter

WHEN a baby is born, the center of his life is self. As soon as he can express himself in the most elementary manner he begins to let you know that *he* must be satisfied, that *his* desires must be fulfilled, *his* demands met.

As far as he is concerned he is the center of the universe —and don't you forget it! If what he wants or needs is not given him, he lets you know in no uncertain manner. If his will is frustrated or denied he will often scream in anger. This is the natural reaction, inherited by one who belongs to a fallen race.

This root of self may be manifested in temper tantrums in an older child when self is thwarted. As he becomes an adult he generally becomes more sophisticated and subtle in trying to get his own way. He will, to a greater or lesser degree, make himself polished and courteous because society will demand it of him. He will be cultured rather than crude; civilized rather than savage. But self will still demand satisfaction. Ego will have to be fed, protected, expressed.

In the baby the demands of self are, of course, unconscious. Moreover, such necessary basic drives as self-preservation are tied in with the infant's reactions. So I am not implying that the described actions and attitudes of the baby are sin, which is a willful rebellion against God. But, springing from a fallen human nature, they lead as naturally into

40

sin as the Jordan River leads into the Dead Sea.

Christ tacitly affirmed this during His Sermon on the Mount. At the time He was not talking to a group that was more sinful than the average. In fact, for the most part, those who were gathered around Him were probably people wanting to live good lives. Yet, clearly implying that humanity is sinful at its roots, He said, "If you then, *who are evil,* know how to give good gifts to your children . . ." (Matt. 7:11, R.S.V.).

He suggests the same idea in His conversation with Nicodemus. He spoke of "that which is born of the flesh." Then, making it plain that He meant men are by inheritance sinful, He avers, "you must be born anew" (John 3:6, 7, R.S.V.). In other words, you must supernaturally become radically different from the kind of person you are by birth; you must be transformed into a different kind of person.

"By Nature Children of Wrath"

A similar affirmation is made by Paul in Ephesians 2:3, when he writes that the Ephesians, who were no different from other people, "were by nature children of wrath." And well known are his words in Romans 7, where he vividly describes his helplessness to overcome sins because he was sinful by nature.

We recall also the words of David: "Behold, I was shapen in iniquity; and in sin did my mother conceive me" (Ps. 51:5); and of Job: "Who can bring a clean thing out of an unclean? not one" (Job 14:4).

Let us use a diagram to illustrate in the simplest manner the condition we have been describing:

We use the heart with the connotation of the desires, feelings, motives, impulses, interests, tendencies, attitudes— those basic qualities and drives that make up the human personality and character.

In this diagram we see the reason why even a baby manifests incipient symptoms of sinfulness. It is because, with self at the center, human nature tends to rebellion against God. Of himself, man has no tendency to do God's will. He wants to do his own. "The outlook of the lower nature [essentially, self] is enmity with God" (Rom. 8:7, N.E.B.).

"I Will Put Enmity"

Any resistance man has to sin is implanted in the heart by God.

> God declares, "I will put enmity." This enmity is not naturally entertained. When man transgressed the divine law, his nature became evil, and he was in harmony, and not at variance, with Satan. There exists naturally no enmity between sinful man and the originator of sin. Both became evil through apostasy. . . . Had not God specially interposed, Satan and man would have entered into an alliance against heaven; and instead of cherishing enmity against Satan, the whole human family would have been united in opposition to God.—*The Great Controversy*, p. 505.
>
> Enmity against Satan is a gift from God.—ELLEN G. WHITE, in *Review and Herald*, May 3, 1906.

God's major channel to the human heart and mind is the conscience.[23] It is an inbuilt faculty, given by God as a means by which He can convey to us His concern over our sins and waywardness.

This faculty, which tells man that some things are right and some wrong, and which nags him when he does wrong, needs to be educated. It can be warped and desensitized. But it is the channel through which God speaks to the soul, prompting the most ignorant heathen, as well as the most enlightened Christian.

God, in concerned love, uses this faculty as a means of trying to bring man back to Himself, so that He can become the center of the life, rather than self. For God knows that man can never be happy, he can never gain the victory over sins, he can never be entrusted with heaven and eternal life, while self is in control. Self, with all its tendencies to evil and troublemaking, must be dethroned and totally subdued.

Unfortunately, when God speaks to us through conscience, we frequently do not recognize what it is He is trying to accomplish in us. For example, God, by means of more of His many channels, is able to speak especially clearly to us on some occasions, and our consciences awaken.

We have a classic example of this in an experience of King David. David had brought about the death of Uriah the Hittite, and then taken his wife for himself. This grave sin benumbed his conscience to a great extent. Finally the auspicious time came, and God sent the prophet Nathan to him with the poignant story of the one little lamb (2 Sam. 12:1-13). And David, condemning himself in the person of a hypothetical rich man, was suddenly brought to recognize himself for what he was. The beautiful penitential Psalm 51 is the result of his awakened conscience.

Let us illustrate God's efforts to get through to us thus, the arrows symbolizing the various means He uses:

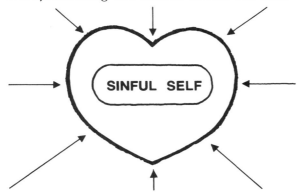

When God succeeds in reaching us, and our consciences become more responsive, we become very much aware of some particular things in our lives that are sinful. These may be sins of the flesh, such as overeating or lust. It may be a dishonest practice. It may be envy, pride, jealousy, gossiping, or a bad temper. Our consciences may begin to accuse us regarding some TV programs we are watching, some books we are reading, or records we are listening to.

"I Must Overcome"

Under these clamorings of conscience, and having a sincere desire to be right with God, we may determine to get rid of these faults. We say to ourselves, "I eat too much. This is sin. I must cut down." Or, "I have been watching 'Everybody Likes Eve' on TV. It is not really a good program for a Christian to view. I am going to cut it out." Or, "I have a temper that is ruining my life. I have got to overcome it."

So we ask God for forgiveness and strength, and set about to correct our faultiness and sins. Consequently, our picture is like this:

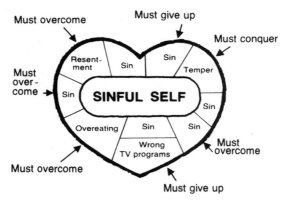

As we look at the diagram, we immediately see the defectiveness of what we are trying to do. "There are many who try to reform by correcting this or that bad habit, and they hope in this way to become Christians, *but they are beginning in the wrong place.* Our first work is with the heart." [24]—*Christ's Object Lessons*, p. 97. (Italics supplied.) To fit the sentence "Our first work is with the heart" with our diagram, we modify it to read, "Our first work is with the *self in* the heart." This is consistent with Ellen White's thought.

Ellen White continues, "The heart must be converted and sanctified."

We may make another application of our diagram by

44

referring to what is another seriously faulty aspect of reformation on the part of some; that which Ellen White refers to as a "patchwork religion." [25] Our diagram helps us visualize the situation.

> The patchwork religion is not of the least value with God. He requires the whole heart. No part of it is to be reserved for the development of hereditary or cultivated tendencies to evil. . . . Many have just such an experience daily, but it is a misrepresentation of the character of Christ.—*The SDA Bible Commentary*, Ellen G. White Comments, on 2 Cor. 5:17, p. 1101.

Trying to Obey Is Not Obedience

The man who attempts to keep the commandments of God merely from a sense of obligation—because he is required to do so—will never enter into the joy of obedience. He does not obey.

He does not obey, because he cannot truly obey. He cannot truly obey from a sense of love even though he really desires to, because self is the center of the life. He is trying to obey—in this case to get rid of certain sins in the life—on the basis of self. Self is trying to discipline self. This is spiritually trying to lift himself by his own bootstraps. [26]

"Self cannot manage self; it is not sufficient for the work. . . . God alone can make and keep us loyal."—*Our High Calling*, p. 215.

We see, then, that when God speaks to us through conscience, He is trying to do far more than lead us to give up particular sins in our lives, important though that is. He wants us to give up self. But, because conscience brings to the fore individual sins, we begin to think in those terms. Right here is where we often miss what God is trying to do, as we observed previously.

> Only when selfishness is dead, when strife for supremacy is banished, when gratitude fills the heart, and love makes fragrant the life—it is only then that Christ is abiding in the soul, and we are recognized as laborers together with God.—*Christ's Object Lessons*, p. 402.
>
> If you cling to self, refusing to yield your will to God, you are choosing death. To sin, wherever found, God is a consuming fire. If you choose sin, and refuse to separate from it, the presence of

God, which consumes sin, must consume you.—*Thoughts From the Mount of Blessing,* p. 62.

Self is difficult to conquer. Human depravity in every form is not easily brought into subjection to the Spirit of Christ. But all should be impressed with the fact that unless this victory is gained through Christ, there is no hope for them. The victory can be gained; for nothing is impossible with God. By His assisting grace, all evil temper, all human depravity, may be overcome.—*Testimonies,* vol. 4, p. 349.

Self is so large in many, ever striving for the mastery. There are those who profess to be followers of Jesus Christ who have never died to self. They have never fallen on the rock and been broken. Until this shall be, they will live unto self, and if they die as they are, it is forever too late for their wrongs to be righted.—*Fundamentals of Christian Education,* p. 284.

Everyone who enters the pearly gates of the city of God will enter there as a conqueror, and his greatest conquest will have been the conquest of self.—*Testimonies,* vol. 9, p. 183.

The question now uppermost in our minds is How do we die to self? The answer is By being born again. In a previous chapter we listed ways one may discover whether he is born again. We shall go on to suggest ways in which the new life may be achieved. But before we think of this pivotal subject, and more clearly and forcibly to accentuate its meaning and depth, we shall think of another aspect of experience that many who live the Christian life go through.

One-hundred-eighty-degree Christians

THERE are degrees of spiritual, or religious, experience, as we all recognize. The Laodicean message suggests a wide range of degrees, temperature-wise: from cold, to lukewarm, to hot.

A recourse to geometry gives us another kind of degree that will help us to see some aspects of the spiritual life:

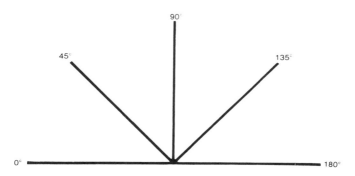

In our illustration, let us take 0 degree as representing the condition of one who has grieved away the Holy Spirit, such as Pharaoh, Esau, Saul, and Judas. The condition of such is hopeless.

The 180-degree mark to the extreme right is used to

47

represent the situation of a person who is fully committed to God. It is not to be understood as bearing any relationship to moral perfection as such; at this point this is not under discussion. It represents only the *attitude* of commitment toward God that prompts us to be totally for Him, and totally to place ourselves, and our all, in His hands. It is fundamentally important that this concept be kept in mind as this and following chapters are studied.

Spiritually speaking, there are people to be found throughout the 180-degree range. In other words, there are people in the church ranging all the way from cold to hot in their commitment attitude, reverting for a moment to the Laodicean picture.

In any case, it seems clear that not all who are Seventh-day Adventists are totally committed to Christ. Ellen G. White writes that "many have accepted the theory of the truth who have had no true conversion" *(Testimonies,* vol. 5, p. 218). She makes an even stronger statement:

> The new birth is a rare experience in this age of the world. This is the reason why there are so many perplexities in the churches. Many, so many, who assume the name of Christ are unsanctified and unholy. They have been baptized, but they were buried alive. Self did not die, and therefore they did not rise to newness of life in Christ.—*The SDA Bible Commentary,* Ellen G. White Comments, on Rom. 6:1-4, p. 1075.

The term "rare" is a strong one. When we think of rare coins, or rare stamps, we recognize that there are not many of that particular type around.

It is true that the words we have just quoted were written many years ago. But can we say the church is in a significantly better spiritual condition today than then? [27]

A Man Named John

Let us now use a hypothetical church member to illustrate the point we wish to make by our diagram. Let us call this imaginary person John.

When we find John he is at a rather low ebb, spiritually. Arbitrarily, for purposes of illustration, we might put him at 45 degrees on our diagram.

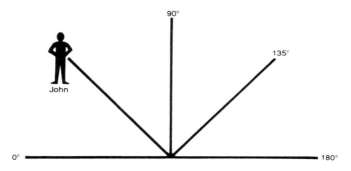

John is a church member "in good and regular standing," but in private is not living up to church standards. For example, he does not pay a faithful tithe. He watches very questionable TV programs, not infrequently on Sabbath. He listens to some pretty far-out music. He practically never studies his Bible, and never opens a Spirit of Prophecy book. These describe only a part of his outward life. Much more could be added to describe the inward.

Then something happens. In some way the Holy Spirit begins to get through to John. Perhaps he had a close call with death in a car accident. Possibly his pastor preached a sermon that brought home to him God's great love for him personally, and the anxiety God has that he be saved. In any case, John moves along in his attitude of commitment to, let us say, 90 degrees.

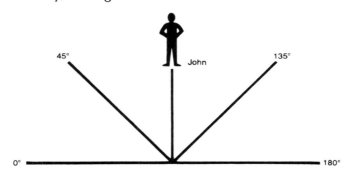

4

John now begins to read his Bible. He quits watching the questionable TV programs. He pays a full tithe, and so on.

The Holy Spirit continues to work with him. And John responds to this wooing in his heart and life until he gets to, shall we say, 170 degrees of commitment.

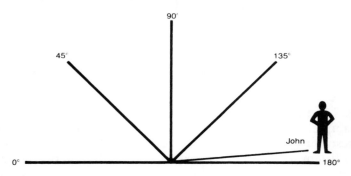

Right here, let us consider a question: The Holy Spirit has been clearly working in John's life, and he has been responding to His love and pleading. But has he been born again if, according to our illustration, he must get to the 180-degree mark of commitment for that experience? The answer is, of course, No. As we described in our heart illustration in the previous chapter, he has been putting a lot of things out of his life that should not be there, and adding a lot of things that should be there. But he has not yet been born again.

Like the rich young ruler (Matt. 19), he has turned in a large degree to Christ. But also, like the rich young ruler, something is still wrong. In the case of the ruler the problem was self-love. "Only one thing he lacked, but that was a vital principle. . . . That he might receive the love of God, his supreme love of self must be surrendered."—*The Desire of Ages*, p. 519.

Another question: Can we say that John has been having a conversion experience?

Before we respond to that question we may wish to consider one or two more ideas.

50

What is the meaning of the term *conversion?* The comparison of a Bible text—Mark 4:12—as rendered by two Bible versions, will help us to discover the answer to this question.

K.J.V.	R.S.V.
That seeing they may see,	So that they may indeed see
and not perceive;	but not perceive,
and hearing they may hear,	and may indeed hear
and not understand;	but not understand;
lest at any time they	lest they
should be converted.	*should turn again.*

The meaning of conversion, then, is simply "a turning."

Two Definitions of Conversion

The Bible shows that in conversion both God and man are involved; in some cases God is described as doing the turning, in others, man. "Turn thou me, and I shall be turned" (Jer. 31:18); "Turn thou us unto thee, O Lord, and we shall be turned" (Lam. 5:21); "turn yourselves, and live ye" (Eze. 18:32); "turn ye, turn ye from your evil ways; for why will ye die, O house of Israel?" (chap. 33:11).

If man has a part in his converting, or turning, it is possible to understand that he might turn only partly toward God, and not fully.

Ellen White seems to use the term *conversion* in two ways. One of these uses indicates the possibility of a partial conversion. She refers to those who have "the hope of salvation . . . without a radical change of heart or reformation of life. Thus superficial conversions abound" *(The Great Controversy,* p. 468). She writes of "half-converted" people *(Testimonies,* vol. 5, p. 114). She describes the need for a "thorough conversion" without which one "may despair of heaven" *(ibid.,* vol. 1, p. 158).

In this context consider some other questions. Is it possible to experience a "superficial" new birth? Can one be half born again? Can the new birth be anything less than thorough and still be a new birth?

Is it possible to answer anything but No to these questions? The new birth is deep, complete.

Jesus in the Central Place

This does not mean that when a person is born again he has a complete experience in the sense that he is totally free of every pull of temptation and sin, that he is free of every propensity to sin. It does not mean instant perfection. This goes without saying. It does mean, as we saw in chapter three, that he becomes "a new creature" with "a new heart" and "a new spirit." It does mean that Jesus has been given the central place in the heart, and that love for the Master reigns in the soul.

To apply our diagram, to have a 45-degree, or 90-degree, or even 179-degree attitude of commitment to God, is not the new birth. These are degrees of conversion, of turning, but not the new birth. According to the illustration we are using, the new birth can only be at 180 degrees.

At this juncture we are reminded of a Spirit of Prophecy statement that has a solemn application to the point we are making:

> There are some who are seeking, always seeking, for the goodly pearl. But they do not make an entire surrender of their wrong habits. They do not die to self that Christ may live in them. Therefore they do not find the precious pearl. They have not overcome unholy ambition and their love for worldly attractions. They do not lift the cross, and follow Christ in the path of self-denial and self-sacrifice. . . . [W]ithout entire surrender there is no rest, no joy. *Almost Christians, yet not fully Christians, they seem near the kingdom of heaven, but they do not enter therein. Almost but not wholly saved means to be not almost but wholly lost.—Selected Messages,* book 1, pp. 399, 400. (Italics supplied.)

In addition to using the term *conversion* in the way we have just seen, Ellen White also uses it in its commonly understood sense, as referring to the new birth:

In the converted person self—

> is not struggling for recognition. . . . If his motives, words, or actions are misunderstood or misrepresented, he takes no offense, but pursues the even tenor of his way. He is kind and thoughtful, humble in his opinion of himself, yet full of hope, always trusting in the mercy and love of God.—*Christ's Object Lessons,* p. 102.

"If He Does Not Resist"

THERE is a statement in *Steps to Christ,* page 27, that struck me very forcibly when I first read it, many years ago. I want to apply it to the diagram illustration used in the previous chapter. In doing so I make an addition to the diagram.

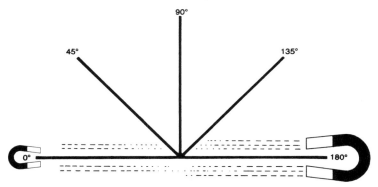

You have noted that the part of the diagram representing the magnet on the right is considerably larger than the other, indicating greater drawing power. The smaller magnet represents the three S's that are pulling us away from God: Satan, self, and sin. The larger magnet represents the influence of the heavenly Father, Jesus, the Holy Spirit, the angels—all the agencies that Heaven uses to attract us to God and to turn us away from self.

Having laid this groundwork, here is the statement that struck me so forcibly: "The sinner may resist this [Christ's] love, . . . but if he does not resist, he will be drawn to Jesus . . ."

There was a time in my early years when I used to picture myself as being almost irresistibly drawn by evil. I felt that it took practically superhuman effort on my part, that I had to sweat blood, as it were, to somehow get to the place of commitment where God would accept me. But the true situation is that in order to thwart what God is doing for me, I actually would have to *resist*, to say, in effect, "No, God, I'm not willing to go as far as You desire. I'm not going to turn *all* of my life over to You. There are some things I insist on keeping, some areas I insist on running myself." [28]

There are other people who feel somewhat as I did regarding finding a relationship with Christ:

> Some seem to feel that they must be on probation and must prove to the Lord that they are reformed, before they can claim His blessing. But these dear souls may claim the blessing even now. They must have His grace, the Spirit of Christ, to help their infirmities, or they cannot form a Christian character. Jesus loves to have us come to Him, just as we are—sinful, helpless, dependent. —*Selected Messages,* book 1, p. 353.

That statement then, from *Steps to Christ,* meant a great deal to me. The greatest drawing power, as I somehow had felt, is not on the 0-degree side. It is on the 180-degree side. "The Lord hath appeared of old unto me, saying, Yea, I have loved thee with an everlasting love; therefore with loving-kindness have I drawn thee" (Jer. 31:3). "I drew them with cords of a man, with bands of love" (Hosea 11:4).

Love Universal and Constant

God's love is as universal, as constant, as the force of gravity that pulls all things on our planet toward its center. We will continue to feel the drawing of that love unless, like a rocket fired from earth toward some other planet, finally getting outside the circle of the earth's attraction,

we get beyond God's love because of persistent sin.
There is another aspect we need to consider.

> God leads His people on, step by step. He brings them up to
> different points calculated to manifest what is in the heart. Some
> endure at one point, but fall off at the next. At every advanced
> point the heart is tested and tried a little closer. If the professed
> people of God find their hearts opposed to this straight work, it
> should convince them that they have a work to do to overcome, if
> they would not be spewed out of the mouth of the Lord. Said the
> angel: "God will bring His work closer and closer to test and prove
> every one of His people." Some are willing to receive one point;
> but when God brings them to another testing point, they shrink
> from it and stand back, because they find that it strikes directly at
> some cherished idol. Here they have opportunity to see what is in
> their hearts that shuts out Jesus. They prize something higher than
> the truth, and their hearts are not prepared to receive Jesus. Indi-
> viduals are tested and proved a length of time to see if they will
> sacrifice their idols and heed the counsel of the True Witness. If
> any will not be purified through obeying the truth, and overcome
> their selfishness, their pride, and evil passions, the angels of God
> have the charge: "They are joined to their idols, let them alone,"
> and they pass on to their work, leaving these with their sinful traits
> unsubdued, to the control of evil angels. Those who come up to
> every point, and stand every test, and overcome, be the price what
> it may, have heeded the counsel of the True Witness, and they will
> receive the latter rain, and thus be fitted for translation.—*Testi-
> monies,* vol. 1, p. 187.

Let us examine this quotation in the context of our
diagram.

In the previous chapter we used a hypothetical man,
John, to illustrate the points we wanted to make. Let us
take him over the same ground again in the setting of the
statement just quoted.

We found church member John at 45 degrees in his
commitment to God. When he was baptized he may have
been at 180 degrees. But gradually he became careless and
let down his guard in certain areas. Slowly he sank to where
we met him, living a Laodicean "tame, lifeless, emotionless
religious experience," as Ellen White describes it.

Of course, there were many things he still adhered to as
an Adventist. For example, let us say he did not drink tea
or coffee. He, of course, gave at least the appearance of

Sabbathkeeping. He went Ingathering faithfully each year. He sent his children to church school. He did those things because he could do them comfortably, without any big struggle with self.*

Then he had his close call with death, or heard that heart-moving sermon. The Holy Spirit began to awaken his conscience, and to show him conditions in his life that needed to be corrected. So he gave up his questionable TV programs, began to pay an honest tithe, started to attend prayer meetings, and so on.

God continued in yearning love to work with his heart, and John continued to respond.

A Battle in the Breast

But let us suppose that at a hypothetical 135-degree point of commitment, conversion, or turning, John is prompted by the Holy Spirit to surrender something that has a strong hold on him. At this point self stiffens its resistance. A battle begins in John's breast in which sin, Satan, and self oppose his conscience, his better judgment, and the Holy Spirit.

Right here John can do one of three things. He can make a decision to follow the promptings of conscience, and the Spirit; he can decide that he is not going to give up that particular sin; or he can take the attitude that if he waits long enough the problem will somehow resolve itself. This is, of course, simply another way of making the second decision by default. In either of the two latter cases he still has his sin.

> We have only to neglect to ally ourselves with the kingdom of light. If we do not co-operate with the heavenly agencies, Satan will take possession of the heart, and will make it his abiding place.— *The Desire of Ages,* p. 324.

What happens if John makes either of the two latter decisions? He does not, under these circumstances, remain at the 135-degree point where the resistance developed. Rather, he begins to slide back toward his old 45-degree position of commitment where everything is comfortable, and he can still be a "good and regular" church member while still doing those things that please self. Satan is once more at ease.

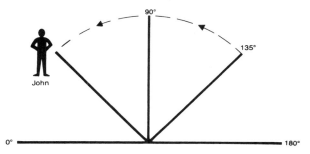

But God does not give John up. On another occasion, when the moment is opportune, the Holy Spirit begins again to appeal to him. Again God's love moves him. Again his conscience is astir. Again he gives up habits and attitudes he had reassumed. And again he is taken over the same ground. Again he comes to 135 degrees of commitment and the sin he met there before. Again the struggle begins.

Joined to His Idols

Suppose that on this occasion John determines to give up that besetting sin. He moves on to, let us say, the 170-degree mark. There he meets the final thing that stands between himself and God and the new birth. A fierce battle rages in his heart. If he fails to make his choice and give himself fully to the control of the Holy Spirit he once again slides back to his old, comfortable, careless, lukewarm position. But not quite. He does not slide back to 45 degrees. It may be 30 degrees, it may be 20 degrees. *It could be zero degrees.* For every time we resist the Holy Spirit we become, to that degree, spiritually desensitized.[30] "If one sin is cherished in the soul, or one wrong practice retained in the life, the whole being is contaminated. The man becomes an instrument of unrighteousness."—*Ibid.*, p. 313.

If John persists in resisting there comes a time when he can no longer respond to Christ's pleadings. Then the words are spoken, "John is joined to his idols, let him alone." And the angels of God pass on, leaving him with his "sinful traits unsubdued, to the control of evil angels."

There is a very important observation I must make here. I have been discussing our imaginary man in the light of the quotation from *Testimonies,* volume 1, page 187. It depicts God taking us over the same ground again and again in order to lead us fully to Himself. Sometimes this takes years, decades, perhaps even a lifetime. *But it does not have to take years.* It could take only moments.

> As soon as we consent to give sin up, to acknowledge our guilt, the barrier is removed between the soul and the Saviour.—*Selected Messages,* book 1, p. 325.
>
> The *moment* we surrender ourselves to God, believing in Him, we have His righteousness.—ELLEN G. WHITE, in *Review and Herald,* July 25, 1899.

How good is God! How eager to gather us, every one, to Himself! How patient He is! How willing immediately to forget the past and place around us the matchless robe of His Son's righteousness—as we are totally willing to do our part.

The Substance and Keynote of Jesus' Teaching

WE HAVE come to the point where we need to consider what Ellen White terms "the substance of the teachings of Christ" (*The Desire of Ages,* p. 523). In another place she refers to it as the keynote of His teaching.

A popular dictionary gives us as the first definition of *substance:* "the real or essential part of anything; essence . . ."

What is it that is the essential element of Christ's message to you and me?

Before we answer this question, let us think awhile of something else. Let us consider something of the "mystery of godliness," that great mystery which the human mind can only partly, and will never fully, understand.

Think of Christ, Creator of all, all-powerful, all-pervading, the Honored of heaven. Surrendering all of this, He leaves the celestial courts, all His glory and power, and becomes encompassed and bound within human flesh, subject to its infirmities, its weaknesses, its temptations.

The Divine Humiliation

He lives as men live, endures as they endure, knows poverty and hardship as the poorest know it. He identifies Himself with the humblest of humanity. That humiliation we can never grasp.

But His descent from the pinnacles of honor and glory

goes far deeper than this. For in Gethsemane He is weighted down with a supernatural horror, an unspeakable woe, such as no man has ever experienced. That horror is because of your sins and mine, the sins of a whole world, that overshadow Him. How awful that experience is. He does not need to go through it. He can shake Himself from it, and go back to heaven. The temptation is strong to do so. The cup trembles in His hands. But He says to the Father as He has said during all His earthly life, "Not my will, but thine be done." And, because He has always been submissive to His Father's will, He goes on to that distillation of sorrow and pain: "unto death, even the death of the cross" (Phil. 2:8).

What the Father Asked, I Ask

Having gone through all of this—for you and me—He says, "I ask of you the same that My Father asked of Me. I did what My Father asked—for you. I must ask you to take the same step."

And so we come to the answer to our question: What was "the substance of the teachings of Christ"?

It was self-surrender.

Christ placed Himself totally in His Father's hands, to be used as the Father saw fit. He taught His followers that they must do this. And you and I must do as He did. We must surrender self to Him, entirely, utterly, completely.[31]

> Entire self-renunciation is required. Unless this takes place, we carry with us the evil that destroys our happiness. But when self is crucified, Christ lives in us, and the power of the Spirit attends our efforts.—*Our High Calling*, p. 21.

In other words, what Jesus Christ, in love, makes mandatory for us, that we might reach the attitude of heart and mind represented by the 180-degree mark of our previous diagram, is a total giving over of ourselves to God, an absolute self-abandonment.

> There are those who profess to be followers of Jesus Christ who have never died to self. They have never fallen on the rock and been broken. Until this shall be, they will live unto self, and if they die as they are, it is forever too late for their wrongs to be righted. —*Fundamentals of Christian Education*, p. 284.

The Substance and Keynote of Jesus' Teaching

What does surrender mean, in concrete terms?

Perhaps, in considering surrender, some of us are inclined to think in terms of *things*. We have previously referred to the incident in which, according to Mark's account, a rich young ruler came running to Christ, so eager was he to find salvation. "Good master," he earnestly inquired, "what good thing shall I do, that I may have eternal life?" (Matt. 19:16).

And, on the surface, Jesus' answer was in terms of "things," but we shall see that it went deeper. Jesus said:

"If thou wilt be perfect, go and sell that thou hast, and give to the poor, and thou shalt have treasure in heaven: and come and follow me" (verse 21).

God Didn't Want Isaac

Consider Abraham on the occasion of the supreme test that God brought to him, the sacrifice of Isaac. That was giving up a "thing," if I may be forgiven for using a word that would be belittling, ordinarily, used in that way. But was God's command simply that Abraham give up Isaac to Him so totally that he would be willing to offer him as a burnt sacrifice? Only in a secondary sense. *What God wanted was not Isaac but Abraham.* And by Abraham's demonstrating his willingness to give up even that which was dearest to himself, he demonstrated that he was indeed surrendering completely to God.[32]

Similarly, Christ was not primarily interested in having the rich young ruler separate himself from his riches. He made that a requirement, apparently, because it was the thing that stood between himself and total surrender to Jesus.[33]

> Man must be emptied of self before he can be, in the fullest sense, a believer in Jesus. When *self* is renounced, *then* the Lord can make man a new creature.—*The Desire of Ages,* p. 280. (Italics supplied.)
>
> We cannot advance in Christian experience until we put away everything that separates us from God.—*Counsels to Parents and Teachers,* p. 329.
>
> The warfare against self is the greatest battle that was ever fought. The yielding of self, surrendering all to the will of God, requires a struggle; but the soul must submit to God before it can be renewed in holiness.—*Steps to Christ,* p. 43.

Self must be crucified before you can overcome in the name of Jesus and receive the reward of the faithful.—*Testimonies,* vol. 4, p. 221.

If sometimes we think in terms of things when we think of surrender to God, we are not completely wrong, of course. Things are definitely included. When I surrender to my Saviour, I must say, in essence, "Jesus, I give my house to You [if I have one]. I dedicate my car to You. I present You with my pocketbook and bank account. I lay in Your hands my family, my friends, my marriage partner, or my marriage partner-to-be. I give You my job, every earthly thing I possess or hope to possess. I am willing to do with them as You will. Only show me.

"And, God, I give You my faculties—my mind, tongue, ears, eyes—my talents, for Your service." [34]

Doing this, and meaning it absolutely, will not be easy. The rich young ruler was not unique among human beings, even though your and my surrender problem may be something other than money.

Things and Attitudes

But difficult though it may be to give up some thing, or things, that is frequently the easiest part of surrender. Harder, and more important, than the surrender of things is the surrender of attitudes. *It is much easier to give up things than attitudes.* But until I give up every wrong attitude I cannot be made a new creature.

Before I can place myself fully, unreservedly, into my Saviour's hands I must repudiate, give over to Him, all self-ishness in my life—jealousy, pride, covetousness, suspicion, faultfinding, touchiness, an overbearing attitude, haughtiness, self-righteousness, the right to anger, bitterness, an unforgiving spirit; any and every ungodly attitude I may have in my heart.

This necessity of giving over to God every wrong attitude was discovered by a woman who greatly desired to be accepted of God. On her knees she earnestly offered herself to Him. But as she prayed she knew that there was one thing, one final attitude, that stood between herself and God. That was a feeling of resentment toward her husband. When she finally won the battle over self, and was able to say, "God, You take over that feeling of resentment," then she had the desired assurance that she was a child of God, and the peace that goes with God's forgiveness. Until a person is willing to go that far, to recognize and admit God's right to every thing, every attitude, *he cannot be born again.*[35]

> When the soul surrenders itself to Christ, a new power takes possession of the new heart. A change is wrought which man can never accomplish for himself. It is a supernatural work, bringing a supernatural element into human nature. The soul that is yielded to Christ becomes His own fortress, which He holds in a revolted world, and He intends that no authority shall be known in it but His own. A soul thus kept in possession by the heavenly agencies is impregnable to the assaults of Satan. But unless we do yield ourselves to the control of Christ, we shall be dominated by the wicked one.—*The Desire of Ages,* p. 324.
>
> If we do not choose to give ourselves fully to God, then we are in darkness. When we make any reserve, we are leaving open a door through which Satan can enter to lead us astray by his temptations. He knows that if he can obscure our vision, so that the eye of faith cannot see God, there will be no barrier against sin.—*Thoughts From the Mount of Blessing,* p. 92.

Often the question is raised How may I know that I have actually surrendered to God?

If I can thoroughly and forthrightly examine my heart in the light of God's Word, and find that it does not condemn me (1 John 3:21), if I have "silence in the soul," peace in the heart, then I may know that I have surrendered to my Saviour.

If I think I have totally committed myself, but do not have peace of heart and conscience, I should ask myself Why. And I should ask God, as I search my heart, to show me why.

If, then, some cherished sin is brought to my attention that I realize I do not really want to give up, I have discovered the source of my problem. I must then earnestly pray, "Lord, make me willing to be made willing to surrender to you."

Actually, when I have surrendered I will know it. For then "the Spirit itself beareth witness with our spirit, that we are the children of God" (Rom. 8:16).

Continual but Complete

Another word needs to be added about total surrender. Self-surrender is a continual process, but it must be complete at every stage. Thus it is a deepening experience.

> The Christian life is one of daily surrender, submission and continual overcoming. . . . If self is surrendered to the divine will, the hand of the Potter will produce a shapely vessel.—*The SDA Bible Commentary,* Ellen G. White Comments, on Isa. 64:8, p. 1154.

Let us illustrate this total yet ongoing process thus. Suppose I decide to give my house, and everything in it, to a dear friend, without strings attached. He comes to the house and looks around. In one room he opens a closet and sees a suit hanging. "Is this mine also?" he asks.

"Oh," I respond, "I hadn't thought of that. But it is still yours."

In the attic he comes across a boxful of valuable books. "How about these? Are these mine also?"

"I had forgotten about them, too. But they are yours to do with as you wish."

Thus, genuine surrender is a complete thing at the time it is made, as far as we know.[36] But there are things in the life that will need to be surrendered that we do not see immediately; unrecognized habits, unconfessed or unrestituted dishonesty, forgotten transgressions, as yet unrevealed weaknesses.[37] But when Jesus brings them to our attention we say, "Yes, Lord, I see what I must do, even though I didn't know about it, or had forgotten it. I shall do what You want."

If this is, and has been, our attitude, we need not be discouraged if today we are impressed that there is something more in our lives that we must give up. Under those circumstances, the call for surrender in a new area tells us that we are growing and that God is calling us to come that much closer to the Saviour.

Meanwhile, it is our duty to pray that God will show us recognizable sins and failings (Ps. 139-23), that we may repent of them and harmonize every detail of our lives with His will. Neglect or refusal to do this makes dangerously possible our shutting ourselves off from God.

The Substance and Keynote of Jesus' Teaching

Some people may be troubled about how to deal with certain specifics in their lives when they surrender. For example, they might wonder, Having surrendered, should I now spend more hours giving Bible studies? Do I have an obligation to give more offerings than I have been giving? Should I sell my house and give some of the proceeds to missions, and rent? There are endless questions that one might ask.

The answer to each such question must be found in each heart and mind. Having given himself, his talents, his time, his possessions, into God's hands, the Christian must not feel under stress about them. He must leave them, unreservedly, in His hands, ask for guidance in every respect, watch for His providences, and follow as the way opens.

Does Surrender Mean Slavery?

There are some who feel that in surrendering to God they will be giving up their individuality, relinquishing their freedom, losing all rights, and becoming slaves without the liberty to think and act for themselves. Nothing could be further from the truth.[38]

Consider. How can a man count himself free when the cravings for self-indulgence—appetite, lust, or some other harmful or destructive habit—rule him? How can he call himself free when he is a slave to an ego that constantly demands satisfaction, attention, protection? How can he be free when every little fancied or real slight or offense can ruin his day? How can he be free when outside the home he has to put on a pleasant mask over the home scowl, and assume a kindly, concerned voice, in place of the home snarl, all the time being fearful that what his family knows him to be will be discovered?[39]

Compare that with the marvelous sense of freedom that comes when you discover you no longer have to wear a mask, to pretend, to protect yourself. You are forgiven by God. You have nothing you feel you must hide. You are at peace. Your sense of guilt is gone. You can be as open as the sky, as transparent as the sunlight. You do not fear exposure, for you can candidly admit your sins, your failings, and say, "Yes, I am a sinner. But Jesus has forgiven me. I shall go on to victory in Him." [40]

That is real freedom. And it comes through surrender to Jesus. [41]

Let us now look further at the person who is not fully yielded to Christ: "Many will be lost while hoping and desiring to be Christians. They do not come to the point of yielding the will to God. They do not now *choose* to be Christians."—*Steps to Christ,* p. 48.

What Accepting Christ Means

There is, then, more to finding a relationship with Jesus than saying, "I believe in Him and I accept Him as my Saviour."

There is more to it than my merely accepting the robe of His righteousness as my own, believing that by this act I stand faultless before God.

I may say, "Come to Jesus just as you are, and He will accept you." This is right. But that coming must be synonymous with complete surrender, and nothing less.

A relationship with Jesus is more than a matter of our accepting Him. (This may be a matter of being deceived by what the old-time, and some modern, theologians called "cheap grace.") It is also a matter of His accepting us. And while He is eager to do so, He can only on condition. "God will accept nothing less than unreserved surrender" *(Review and Herald,* May 16, 1907).

There is great and joyful assurance in such words as, "We are not to be anxious about what Christ and God think of us, but about what God thinks of Christ, our Substitute."—*Selected Messages,* book two, pp. 32-33. But on what basis do these words apply for us? We are holding on to a false hope if we do not understand and act within the context in which the statement is made. Before she makes the statement Ellen White writes, *"When we surrender* ourselves wholly to God, and fully believe, the blood of Christ cleanses from all sin." And almost immediately after the statement in question, she observes, "The Lord shows, to the repenting, believing one, that Christ *accepts the surrender of the soul,* to be *molded* and *fashioned* after His own likeness." (Italics supplied.)

Thus it is the *totally surrendered one* who is to trust to what God thinks of his Substitute. This point we must not miss.

There are certain steps that must be taken for a person to become accepted by God. First, as we have seen, must come complete surrender. This permits Jesus to justify the sinner, to impute to him His own righteousness so that he is regarded by the Father as if he had never sinned. *Then* begins the process of sanctification, or the impartation of Christ's life to him.

Note these two statements carefully:

> God requires the entire surrender of the heart, *before* justification can take place.—*Ibid.,* book 1, p. 366.
> Justification means the saving of a soul from perdition, that he may obtain sanctification, and through sanctification, the life of heaven. Justification means that the conscience, purged from dead works, is placed where it can receive the blessings of sanctification.—*The SDA Bible Commentary,* Ellen G. White Comments, on 1 Thess. 4:3, p. 908.

Pregnant With Eternal Consequences

The implications of these quotations are very serious, pregnant with eternal consequences:

The person who is not completely yielded to Christ cannot be justified.

The person who is not justified cannot be sanctified, or "reach perfection of holiness" (Rom. 5:9, 10; 2 Cor. 7:2, *Jerusalem Bible*).

Without this experience of justification and ongoing sanctification, "no man shall see the Lord" (Heb. 12:14).

"The Potter cannot mold and fashion unto honor that which has never been placed in His hands."—*Ibid.,* Ellen G. White Comments, on Isa. 64:8, p. 1154.

Knowing that he has sins in his life that he must overcome, an unsurrendered man, even though he may sincerely believe Jesus is his Saviour, keeps struggling with those sins year after year, seeking to overcome hereditary and cultivated tendencies to evil that he knows are sinful, destructive of faith and hope, which weaken his Christian witness, and stand between himself and heaven.

After ten, twenty, thirty years of struggle he has not been able to get rid of them. But he reasons grimly to himself, "Sanctification *is* the work of a lifetime."

But the frightening fact is, that unless he has an attitude of complete surrender to Jesus, he has not even been justified. *And the process of sanctification has not even begun.*

Let us go to our 180-degree diagram once more to illustrate our point graphically:

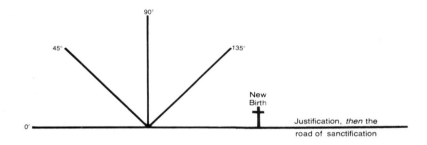

Unless one is totally surrendered, he cannot possibly overcome his sins. But "let no one despair of gaining the victory. Victory is sure when self is surrendered to God."— *Ibid.,* Ellen G. White Comments, on Gen. 32:24, p. 1095.

> The Lord can do nothing toward the recovery of man until, convinced of his own weakness, and stripped of all self-sufficiency, he yields himself to the control of God. Then he can receive the gift that God is waiting to bestow.—*The Desire of Ages,* p. 300.
>
> If we will trust Him, and commit our ways to Him, He will direct our steps in the very path that will result in our obtaining the victory over every evil passion, and every trait of character that is unlike the character of our divine Pattern.—*Our High Calling,* p. 316.

In chapter five (page 41) we used a diagram of a heart to illustrate man's fundamental problem, which is not individual sins and faults, but self. At this point we can go back to that illustration and add another point.

We saw in chapter five that when the Spirit of God begins

to speak to the heart our awakened consciences make us think in terms of specific sins in our lives. So we begin to work on those sins. But, as we have discussed in this chapter, it is not sins, or things, that God wants. It is the heart, with self dethroned.

But it goes further than that. God does not want the heart to renovate it. He wants to replace it entirely by a new heart. "A new heart I will give you, and a new spirit I will put within you; and I will take out of your flesh the heart of stone and give you a heart of flesh. And I will put my spirit within you, and cause you to walk in my statutes and be careful to observe my ordinances" (Eze. 36:26, 27, R.S.V.). "Therefore if any man be in Christ, he is a new creature: old things are passed away; behold, all things are become new" (2 Cor. 5:17).

What does this mean? When we defined what we understood by the heart, in chapter five, we stated it meant the desires, feelings, motives, impulses, interests, tendencies, attitudes. So the new birth—for this, of course, is what we are discussing—results in new desires, new feelings, motives, impulses, interests, tendencies, attitudes.

Same Man, but Different

We have described a perpetual miracle. That God can take a man, a being with a will of his own, with certain educational, environmental, and hereditary set of character, and make an altogether different man of him is unbelievable, humanly speaking. The face is the same, the voice is the same, the brain cells are the same, the abilities are the same, the over-all personality is readily recognizable. It is the same man, yet it is *not* the same man. The characteristics that count in him are different. His thinking and attitudes, his likes and dislikes, are different. There is a new direction to his ambitions.

> When the Spirit of God takes possession of the heart, it transforms the life. Sinful thoughts are put away, evil deeds are renounced; love, humility, and peace take the place of anger, envy, and strife. Joy takes the place of sadness, and the countenance reflects the light of heaven. No one sees the hand that lifts the

burden, or beholds the light descend from the courts above. The blessing comes when by faith the soul surrenders itself to God. Then that power which no human eye can see creates a new being in the image of God.—*The Desire of Ages*, p. 173.

This change is brought about because there is a union of divinity (the indwelling Christ) with our humanity. Through this union we may live the Christ life.

The experience of the new birth may be depicted by the right-hand portion of the diagram below. At justification (see chap. 17) and the new birth, symbolized by baptism (Rom. 6:4, 5), the pardoned sinner receives the new heart. The life is then directed from within by the indwelling Christ.

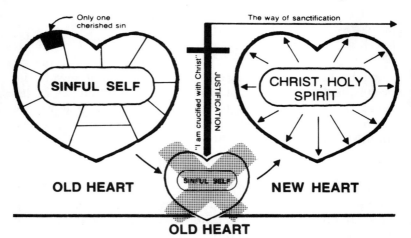

But baptism does not automatically mean that a person is born again. "Many, so many, who assume the name of Christ, are unsanctified and unholy. They have been baptized, *but they were buried alive*. Self did not die, and therefore they did not rise to newness of life in Christ."—*The SDA Bible Commentary*, Ellen G. White Comments, on Rom. 6:1-4, p. 1075. (Italics supplied.) They arose from the baptismal font with the same hearts they possessed before they were immersed. And just one *cherished* sin will have this result.

But I Don't Want to Surrender!

SELF-SURRENDER, as we have seen, is the answer to finding God, forgiveness, peace, victory, and heaven.

But the question many ask is *How* am I to surrender? And, just as important with many, How do I become so I *want* to surrender? For the truth is, some say, I have no real desire to give myself to God. Candidly, if my chances for salvation depend on how I feel toward God, I guess I'm lost. If desire is a motivation, I seem to have none. I seem to be drained of all desire, all will, to be saved. I feel spiritually numb.[42]

All I have, they may add, is an intellectual realization that if I do not surrender I can't be saved. Now tell me, they continue, how can a person who has no desire to surrender, surrender?

Let's look at it this way: Here is a man who has been caught in a terrible blizzard somewhere on the prairies. The temperature has plummeted to twenty degrees below zero, and as he struggles through the wind-driven snow toward home the bitter cold begins to penetrate into his very bones, it seems.

But after a time he begins to realize that he doesn't feel the cold quite as much any more. Also, a temptation to sleep is creeping over him. How delightful it would be just to lie down, be covered with a white blanket of snow, and give

71

way to pleasant drowsiness. The temptation becomes almost overwhelming.

But behind the desire to sleep, reason says, You can't sleep! If you do, you die! You must go on!

So the man struggles on in spite of the desire to quit, until he gets home.

It was not his feelings that drove him to safety. Feelings said, Sleep! You don't feel like going on. Quit!

But reason said, You don't want to die. You must live! You must keep going!

And, in spite of the way he felt, the man obeyed reason.

What is the spiritual lesson for us here? As the man in the blizzard struggled toward home in spite of all feeling, so the person who only intellectually realizes he needs Christ, must strive to find Him, or he is lost.

So again we ask the question How may I, with merely an intellectual realization of my need, get to the place where I can surrender to God?

No Answers in Thirty Minutes

We live in a day when we want quick, easy answers to our questions. We want TV solutions to our problems—answers in the next thirty minutes, with time out for commercials. We want answers right now so we can get it over with and get on with something else.

But we must know this from the very beginning: God does not always give a quick answer. And He never gives, He cannot give, a quick, easy answer to the question we have just posed. Sin is too pervasive, too deep-seated, too profound a problem, to deal with in thirty minutes. Remember, Christ had to spend thirty years here on earth to make the solution available. And only as we look long and thoughtfully at the cross can we begin to realize what the answer to our question is.

To begin to find an answer to our question, let us take a look at a text—John 15:5. The last part reads, "Without me ye can do nothing."

In context, Jesus is telling His disciples that they are branches dependent upon the vine—Himself—for spiritual life and fruit bearing. But also, they could not become part of the vine except as He grafted them in, as it were.

For the sinner to be spiritually grafted in to Jesus, there are a number of steps that he must take. First, he must repent.

But he cannot repent of himself. Repentance comes from Christ. "God exalted him [Jesus] . . . to give repentance to Israel" (Acts 5:31, R.S.V.).[43]

Before he can be grafted in to Christ, the sinner must be forgiven of his sins. The same text tells us that Jesus also gives "forgiveness of sins."

Also, before he can be grafted in he must be justified, accepted as righteous, by the Father. This also comes through Jesus. We are "justified by his grace as a gift, through the redemption which is in Christ Jesus" (Rom. 3:24, R.S.V.).

The Christian receives "eternal life [only] by Jesus Christ our Lord" (chap. 5:21).

Christ is able "to save absolutely those who approach God through Him" (Heb. 7:25, N.E.B.), and there is no other way to get to the Father but by Him (John 14:6).

Through Christ, and only through Christ, can we have real victory in our lives: "I can do all things through Christ which strengtheneth me" (Phil. 4:13).

And there is absolutely no other way by which we may be saved (Acts 4:12).

As we ponder these thoughts a light begins to dawn in our minds: We cannot do anything of ourselves. We cannot repent of our sins. We cannot come to God. We cannot surrender. We cannot have victory over our sins. Moreover life, real life, freedom, rest, and all other worthwhile blessings, come through Jesus.

Then we remember another text, a key text, that puts it all together: "This is life eternal, that they might know thee the only true God, and Jesus Christ, whom thou hast sent" (John 17:3).

We Had Better Know Jesus

If this is so, if all things come from Him, *then we had better get to know Jesus.* For we have begun to see that the answer to our great dilemma is Jesus. "Acquaint now thyself with him . . .: thereby good shall come unto thee" (Job 22:21).

So we ask, How do we become acquainted with Him?

By setting out to find Him, just as the man in the blizzard, with only reason to tell him to struggle on, persisted until he arrived home.

This one fact we must recognize: There must be effort on our part. We must start by responding to reason, just as the man in the blizzard put forth every effort in response to reason. For him merely to hope for his life to be preserved while he did nothing would have been fatal. So "he who does nothing but wait to be compelled by some supernatural agency, will wait on in lethargy and darkness."—ELLEN G. WHITE, in *Review and Herald,* July 17, 1888."

"If the youth will *seek* Christ, He will make their efforts effectual."—*Messages to Young People,* p. 18. And not only will the efforts of youth to seek Christ be made effectual; there is no age limit to seeking God.

In the same book Mrs. White writes of "deliberately and intelligently" accepting Christ's terms of salvation (page 30). This is done by diligently searching them out, by seeking to understand them, and following them closely. "If we seek God with earnestness, He will impress us by His Holy Spirit" (ELLEN G. WHITE, in *Review and Herald,* Oct. 31, 1912).[45]

Where may one search for Christ?

"Search the scriptures," said Christ, ". . . they are they which testify of me" (John 5:39). The Scriptures, said Paul, "are able to make thee wise unto salvation" (2 Tim. 3:15).

These are vitally important words. *Do not slide over them casually.* If you do you may almost as well stop reading right here. For this is essentially the whole answer to our question. We find Jesus by going to where He is revealed. That is in His Word.

Immediately after her warning against waiting for a super-naturally compelling power to arouse us, quoted above, Ellen White says, telling how to escape from lethargy and darkness, "God has given us His word. God speaks in unmistakable language to your soul. Is not the word of His mouth sufficient to show you your duty, and to urge its fulfillment?"

Nor is it sufficient to take the word of others regarding

the Bible's teachings: "We should not take the testimony of any man as to what the Scriptures teach, but should study the words of God for ourselves."—*Steps to Christ*, p. 89.

The Bible, then, is the channel by which God has ordained that His Son shall be found.[45] One who does not take these words seriously will have taken an attitude that makes it hard, if not impossible, for God really to get through to him with the information he must have. "The Bible and the soul were made one for the other."—*Signs of the Times*, Aug. 20, 1894.

Yet it seems that so few, even of Adventists, really try to get to know Jesus at all. In fact, most seem to ignore Him, if a survey that was made a while back paints a typical picture. The survey showed that in the churches surveyed, only one Adventist in four did any studying of their Bibles at all.[47]

Not Found Casually

We will not find what we need by a casual, haphazard seeking. "And ye shall seek me, and find me, when ye shall search for me with all your heart" (Jer. 29:13).

> There must be earnest study and close investigation [of Scriptures]. Sharp, clear perception of truth will never be the reward of indolence. No earthly blessing can be obtained without earnest, patient, persevering effort. . . . And we cannot expect to gain spiritual knowledge without earnest toil. . . . No halfhearted, indifferent work will avail. It is essential for old and young, not only to read God's word, but to study it with wholehearted earnestness, praying and searching for truth as for hidden treasure. Those who do this will be rewarded, for Christ will quicken the understanding.
>
> Our salvation depends on a knowledge of the truth contained in the Scriptures.—*Christ's Object Lessons*, p. 111.

In our search we must sincerely ask the Holy Spirit to make what we study meaningful, and to apply it to our hearts. This is vitally important.

> Without the Spirit of God a knowledge of His word is of no avail. The theory of truth, unaccompanied by the Holy Spirit, cannot quicken the soul or sanctify the heart. One may be familiar with the commands and promises of the Bible; but unless the Spirit of God sets the truth home, the character will not be transformed.— *Ibid.*, p. 408.
>
> When you search the Scriptures with an earnest desire to learn

> the truth, God will breathe His Spirit into your heart and impress your mind with the light of His word.—*Testimonies,* vol. 4, p. 499.

Don't keep looking for something sudden, dramatic, earth-shaking, world-changing, to take place.

There are those who see that God has changed the lives of others, and want what they have. They begin to seek. Days or weeks pass, and nothing unusual seems to be happening. They don't feel any different. So they become discouraged and let it all go.

Please know, God usually comes to us like the quiet tide rather than like a violent tidal wave. Gradually, almost imperceptibly, the tide sweeps in, slowly conquering the sand and shore. And one may watch for several minutes before he is sure the tide is indeed coming in.

> By an agency as unseen as the wind, Christ is constantly working upon the heart. Little by little, perhaps unconsciously to the receiver, impressions are made that tend to draw the soul to Christ. These may be received through meditating upon Him, through reading the Scriptures, or through hearing the word from the living preacher. Suddenly, as the Spirit comes with more direct appeal, the soul gladly surrenders itself to Jesus. By many this is called sudden conversion; but it is the result of long wooing by the Spirit of God —a patient, protracted process.—*The Desire of Ages,* p. 172.

We do our part in preparation by immersing ourselves in the Word, by seeking to absorb it as a sponge absorbs water, by becoming familiar with it so that we understand the way God speaks.[48]

The Dull Becomes Fascinating

At first we may find the Bible uninteresting and hard to understand. But perseverance will change all of that. As we permit the Holy Spirit to work, truths will begin to fall into place; the seemingly dull will become interesting, even fascinating.[49]

What should be studied? Those parts of the Bible that unfold God's way of salvation. The first eight chapters of Romans, especially chapters three to eight. The books of Galatians and Ephesians. The Sermon on the Mount.

What we have been saying about the vital necessity of studying the Bible applies with equal force to the Spirit of

Prophecy writings. As Seventh-day Adventists we believe that Ellen G. White's books are God's special messages for those who live in earth's last days. And in her books *Steps to Christ, Thoughts From the Mount of Blessing, Christ's Object Lessons,* and *The Desire of Ages* especially, we find the way to the Saviour beautifully unfolded. "As they [those who hunger for Jesus] feed upon His word, they find that it is spirit and life. The word destroys the natural, earthly nature, and imparts a new life in Christ Jesus."—*Ibid.,* p. 391.[50]

As you study and seek, entertain a humble expectation that God will help. Remember, He does not mock us; He will not play with us. He is more eager that we find Him than we can ever be. When our hearts are properly prepared, He will come in a direct way.

When He makes the loving invitation, respond immediately. It is safe to let go of self and every worldly support, and take the hand of Him who guides the millions of worlds in His vast universe.

> Jesus loves to have us come to Him just as we are, sinful, helpless, dependent. We may come with all our weakness, our folly, our sinfulness, and fall at His feet in penitence. It is His glory to encircle us in the arms of His love, and to bind up our wounds, to cleanse us from all impurity.—*Steps to Christ,* p. 52.

Why does He accept sinners in their sinful condition?

> He is waiting to strip them of their garments stained and polluted with sin, and to put upon them the white robes of righteousness; He bids them live and not die.—*Ibid.,* p. 53.

He wants to pardon and justify.

Study With Others

Experience has shown that one very helpful way to find a relationship with Christ is to spend time studying with others who know Him and who desire to talk of Him and what He has done for them.

> Let small companies assemble in the evening, at noon, or in the early morning to study the Bible. Let them have a season of prayer, that they may be strengthened, enlightened, and sanctified by the Holy Spirit.—*Testimonies,* vol. 7, p. 195.

Not only must the Scriptures be searched to find Christ;

they must be habitually searched to retain Him. This is the intent of John 6:54. The Greek verb tense conveys the idea, "Whoever continues to eat my flesh and drink my blood, has eternal life."

"To eat the flesh and drink the blood of Christ is to receive Him as a personal Saviour, believing that He forgives our sins, and that we are complete in Him."—*The Desire of Ages,* p. 389.

The process of partaking of Christ is the practice of searching and absorbing the truths of Scripture. And this must be done daily, as we must partake of physical food daily. If we do not do this we will become spiritually weak and listless, perhaps without realizing why.

> As our physical life is sustained by food, so our spiritual life is sustained by the word of God. And every soul is to receive life from God's word for himself. As we must eat for ourselves in order to receive nourishment, so we must receive the word for ourselves. We are not to obtain it merely through the medium of another's mind. We should carefully study the Bible, asking God for the aid of the Holy Spirit, that we may understand His word.—*Ibid.,* p. 390.

Why Blessings Are Lost

Perhaps the greatest reason why the blessed experience gained during revival meetings or following an inspiring sermon is lost is because we do not sustain the blessing by continuing in the Word that we have heard preached. During those meetings the Holy Spirit sometimes speaks forcefully to our hearts. We bask in that blessing and leave the meetings with a determination to retain it. But unless we act to do so, we will lose it. God's blessings can be retained only as we watch and pray and go continually to the Source from which they came. That Source is Jesus Christ as found in His Word.

To find the gateway to surrender, then, we must deliberately and intelligently go to where we can be shown the way—the Bible and the writings of Ellen G. White. We must patiently, perseveringly, prayerfully, earnestly, fill our minds and hearts with those passages and pages that show us the way to Jesus Christ. As we do this we need not fear that God will not respond to our seeking. He sees every soul who is searching for Him a great way off. "Him that cometh to me I will in no wise cast out" (John 6:37).

Let this be your prayer, "Take everything from me, let me lose property, worldly honor, everything, but let Thy presence be with me." It is safe to commit the keeping of the soul to God, who reigns over all heaven and earth.—*Special Testimonies to Ministers,* series A, no. 1, p. 8.

The Soul's Controlling Faculty

LET us spend a little time with our hypothetical church member, John, once more. In chapter six we found him in a situation of conflict. There, following an experience that awakened him to his spiritual needs, the Holy Spirit was able to convict him of sin, and he began to put specific sins out of his life. Then, at a certain point, we suggested that he was faced with a sinful practice that had a very strong hold on him. Self began to stiffen its resistance, and as a result, a strong battle began in John's heart.

Right here, let us stop to analyze the faculties involved in this battle.

1. **Intellect,** by which we mean that faculty that perceives, understands, judges, and reasons.

2. **Sensibilities,** by which we mean the desires, feelings, emotions, impulses, and others.

3. **Will,** the faculty of decision, of choice.

Let us see how these faculties are involved in the struggle going on in John's heart.

Let us assume that the process begins with the faculty of intellect. As the Holy Spirit works with John, He brings to his attention, to his faculty of perception, the certain sin around which the battle rages. When John understands the situation, reason tells him that he ought to rid himself of the sin.

But already his sensibilities faculty—his desires, emotions, impulses—has reacted. In no uncertain manner it gives notice that it is utterly against surrendering the practice, and that it will fight the idea to the bitter end.

Reason says, That habit is a barrier between you and Jesus. Unless you are willing to give it up you can never be born again. You can never see heaven unless it is surrendered.

But desire argues, Why should you be so foolish as to throw away a practice you enjoy so much? That is one of the things you get the most satisfaction from. If you keep on giving up all those things to Jesus as you have, pretty soon your life will be about as bleak and empty as a barren island.

So reason and logic urge John in one direction, and feelings and desires in another.

Resolving the Battle

How is the battle to be resolved? In one way only; by the will. The will must go into action and make a decision.[51]

In every action of our lives, a hundred times a day, this process goes on, in moral and nonmoral situations. Many times the process is so brief, so automatic, so unimportant, that we do not recognize it. Sometimes it is fraught with eternal consequences, such as that which we have projected for our imaginary John.

There is another important factor that must be recognized here: The human will is free, but weak, limited, and sin-infected.[52] Consequently, a man cannot save himself from sin, for in order to do this he must use his will. But his will is the very seat of the deadly infection. It is naturally directed toward evil rather than good. As Paul observed, the unregenerate, unconsecrated man is "taken captive by . . . [Satan] at his will" (2 Tim. 2:26). "If we were left to follow our own inclinations, to go just where our will would lead us, we should fall into Satan's ranks and become possessors of his attributes."—*The Desire of Ages*, p. 329. "It is through the will that sin retains its hold upon us."—*With God at Dawn*, p. 251.

At this point we are in a quandary. It is the will that decides whether we are going to hold on to sin or expel it from the soul. *But* the natural will is inclined to do Satan's will. Moreover, it is too weak to do good, even when we desire to turn it in that direction. "For to will is present with me," Paul exclaimed, "but how to perform that which is good I find not" (Rom. 7:18). Thus, to try to do good on our own is contrary to nature. It is self-destructing. It is a grinding machine wearing itself away.

The counteraction of such a situation is illustrated by the lively little girl who frequently got into mischief. Mother, as often as she felt it imperative, would discipline her daughter. But it seemed to do little good.

On one occasion, after little Patsy had been especially annoying, mother gave her a severe lecture. Patsy began to realize the nature of her misconduct, became repentant, and promised to be a good girl.

For a time everything went well. Then mother began to notice Patsy slipping back to her old ways again.

Hoping that a reminder of her promise would be enough to keep Patsy in line, mother said, "Patsy, you have been a good girl for a while. Why don't you stay that way?"

"Oh, Mother," was the response, "I can't, because it makes me so tired."

This is the way it is when we try to overcome our sins on our own. We become weary of the tension, of the constant battle that we don't particularly desire to fight. We become tired and, after a time, we quit.

Nevertheless, it is possible for a person to obey God without tension, without a feeling that he must obey, rather than wanting to obey.

A Pivotal Area

Right here is a vitally important, indeed, a pivotal, area in our answer to the question we asked in the previous chapter, How am I to surrender self to God?

Many are inquiring, *"How* am I to make the surrender of myself to God?" You desire to give yourself to Him, but you are weak in moral power, in slavery to doubt, and controlled by the habits of your life of sin. . . . The knowledge of your broken promises and forfeited pledges weakens your confidence in your own sincerity, and causes you to feel that God cannot accept you; but you need not despair. What you need to understand is the true force of the will. This is the governing power in the nature of man, the power of decision, or of choice.—*Steps to Christ,* p. 47.

Then Ellen White makes this exceedingly significant statement: "Everything depends on the right action of the will."—*Ibid.*

Elsewhere, she writes:

> The power of choice God has given to men; it is theirs to exercise. You cannot change your heart, you cannot of yourself give to God its affections; but you can *choose* to serve Him. You can give Him your will; He will then work in you to will and to do according to His good pleasure. Thus your whole nature will be brought under the control of the Spirit of Christ; your affections will be centered upon Him, your thoughts will be in harmony with Him.—*Ibid.*

Picture a giant electromagnetic crane, designed to lift scrap iron. The operator swings the crane around and drops the head upon the metal. But nothing happens. Or perhaps two or three pounds of metal are attracted to it.

Then the operator throws a switch that permits electricity to flow to the device. Now when he manipulates his levers and lifts the electromagnet hundreds of pounds of iron are held by it.

The vast difference between the head that had no power and the one that could lift hundreds of pounds was in the electric current. Flowing through the wire around the core of the device, the current created a powerful magnet.

Energizing the Will

So with the human will. Of itself it has little or no power to deal effectively with sin, or to do God's will. But when the Holy Spirit flows into the life the divine will energizes the human. Then the individual can do all things through Christ who strengthens him. "As the will of man co-operates with the will of God, it becomes omnipotent."—*Christ's Object Lessons,* p. 333.

Man, then, cannot of himself will to spurn evil and do right. He cannot do this any more than the Ethiopian can change his skin or the leopard his spots. But he can will to place his will under the control of God.

> In the work of redemption there is no compulsion. No external force is employed. Under the influence of the Spirit of God, man is left free to choose whom he will serve. In the change that takes place when the soul surrenders to Christ, there is the highest sense of freedom. The expulsion of sin is the act of the soul itself. True we have no power to free ourselves from Satan's control; but when we desire to be set free from sin, and in our great need cry out for a power out of and above ourselves, the powers of the soul are imbued with the divine energy of the Holy Spirit, and they obey the dictates of the will in fulfilling the will of God.—*The Desire of Ages*, p. 466.

We take a moment to note an essential thought in this quotation: "When we desire to be set free from sin," and cry out for deliverance, *then* the power comes to energize the will. If we do not really desire, if we have reservations and do not genuinely want to surrender, our wills will not be strengthened to expel sin from the soul. A great many people *want* to have a victorious relationship with Christ, but they do not *will* to have one. "Until we are willing, the transforming grace of God cannot be manifest upon us."—*Thoughts From the Mount of Blessing*, p. 143.[58]

> Christ is ready to set us free from sin, but He does not force the will; and if by persistent transgression the will itself is wholly bent on evil, and we do not *desire* to be set free, if we *will* not accept His grace, what more can He do? We have destroyed ourselves by our determined rejection of His love.—*Steps to Christ*, p. 34.

> Let a solemn, unalterable purpose take possession of you, and resolve in the strength and grace of God, that henceforth you will live for Him, and that no earthly consideration shall persuade you to disown the divine law of ten commandments.—*The Faith I Live By*, p. 82.

This transaction, then, is not a passive one on our part. It is not simply "God, You take my will. I merely allow You to do so." It is an active transaction: "God, here is my will, I hand it to You. Please take it and do what needs to be done. I will that Your will be done in me. I will surrender to You, to cooperate fully with You."

When this decision is made the soul has found the answer to the question How do I surrender self to God?

Faith and an Orange

"LOVE is the greatest thing in the world," said A. J. Gordon, "but faith is the first." If this is so, then faith should have been the theme of our first chapter. However, the development of our approach required that we leave it until now.

A. J. Gordon was quite correct. It is as faith glimmers in the soul, causing an individual to look to Jesus, that he is on the threshold of the Christian life. When he surrenders to Christ, the Holy Spirit takes possession of the life and begins to transform it. Then comes the fruit of the Spirit: "love, joy, peace, patience, kindness, goodness, faithfulness, gentleness, self-control" (Gal. 5:22, R.S.V.).

Faith is absolutely necessary for the Christian. We are accepted by God only on the basis of the righteousness that is ours by our exercise of faith (Rom. 4:4-6). It is our faith in Christ that makes it possible for Him to carry on the work of sanctification in our lives (Acts 26:18). We cannot even approach God in prayer without at least an atom of faith (Heb. 11:6).

But many who would live the Christian life seem to see faith as something that is doled out sparingly by God to special people. To some it is a sort of illusory, mysterious concept requiring one to be a learned theologian to understand, and a mystic or visionary, or perhaps a very simple person, to possess. Again, others see faith as a sort of magical attribute that somehow enables its possessor to have unusual experiences.

The Simplicity of Faith

Because we have these, and other, incorrect ideas of faith, too many Christians fail to grasp what Ellen White calls "the simplicity of true faith" *(Messages to Young People,* p. 111).

To me, one of the best illustrations of this simple faith we are attempting to describe is given by I. H. Evans, a former vice-president of the General Conference.

In his capacity as a vice-president Elder Evans had to do a great deal of traveling. Each time he returned home he had the practice of taking a small gift to each of his children, so they got into the habit of expecting it.

Arriving home from one trip late at night, he went to bed without awakening the children to let them know he had returned.

The next morning he was out in his yard when his little boy came running toward him shouting, "Hello, Daddy! Hello, Daddy!"

Elder Evans picked up his son and greeted him, then the boy asked, "Daddy, what did you bring me this time?"

"I brought you an orange," was the response. (That was in days when oranges were not as readily available in certain areas as now.)

The boy slid out of his father's arms, shouting, "I have an orange! I have an orange!"

His son's unquestioning acceptance of his word struck Elder Evans so forcefully that he asked, "Let me see your orange."

His eyes beginning to fill with tears, the lad held out his empty hands, and asked, "Don't I have an orange?"

Ashamed at having raised a doubt in his little son's mind, Elder Evans assured him, "Yes, you have; of course you have. It is in my bag in the closet."

And away the boy ran toward the house, shouting at the top of his voice, "I have an orange! I have an orange! I have an orange!"

Possessed by Faith

Then Elder Evans asks, "How could that little lad shout with joy when he had not seen the orange, or smelled it, and did not know where it was? Because of his faith in my word. He believed; his faith caused him to possess."—Cited in *The Preacher and His Preaching*, pp. 86, 87.

That is faith, simple faith. The type of faith that all must possess in God. It is trustingly believing God, who cannot lie, and who does not deceive, and acting upon that belief.

Ellen White describes two incidents in her experience that illustrate "the simplicity of true faith."

She had a sister, named Elizabeth, who seemed not to be able to understand faith. She was suffering from poor health, so Mrs. White wrote her saying, "Ask anything you will, that is in my power to obtain, to make you comfortable, and you shall have it."

Believing what Ellen said, Elizabeth wrote of a wheel chair she thought would be helpful. Then she had a chair selected before she answered Ellen's letter, confident that her sister would pay for it.

"How is it," Mrs. White observed, "that she could believe my word, and yet could not believe in the promises of Jesus?" —In *Review and Herald*, March 19, 1889.

In the same issue she tells of an Adventist sister in Oakland, California, who had been complaining of a lack of faith in God. This woman on one occasion reminded Mrs. White that she had promised to give her a copy of *The Testimonies*, volume four, when it was revised and enlarged.

"Did I?" Mrs. White asked. "And did you really believe I meant it?"

"Certainly," was the reply.

"Why did you think so?" Sister White responded. "Is it not strange that you should think I would do that, simply because I promised you?"

The woman looked at her in astonishment. Then Mrs. White made her point. "How is it," she asked, "that you can trust in a promise of mine, but cannot trust your heavenly Father's word? How is it that you can have faith in a poor, fallible mortal, and cannot rely upon the unchangeable God? I had forgotten my promise; but God never forgets. Why can't you take Him at His word, as you take me at my word?"

A Definition of Faith

These three incidents help us to formulate a definition of faith: Faith is complete belief in God, a trustful expectation that He will fulfill His promises, and confident opening of the heart and hands to receive what He gives. Faith is not faith without all three of these elements.

Many say they believe in God, but it turns out to be simply an intellectual credence. They have been taught there is a God, or they see evidence in the Bible, in nature, science, or in experience, that He exists. But their belief stops right there.

Faith goes beyond this. It includes the confident expectation that He will, for example, give us full victory over our sins, that He will supply the love for others we are lacking, that He will help us overcome envy, pride, malice, jealousy, a quick temper, and every other failing. It is an attitude that leads us to accept undoubtingly His promise that He will provide for our every need and help us in every emergency when we are fully committed and fully obedient to Him. "True faith rests on the promises contained in the Word of God, and those only who obey that Word can claim its glorious promises."—*Early Writings*, pp. 72, 73.

Faith is that attitude of utter willingness toward God that causes us to open our hearts and minds so that He can do for us what He wants to do. Faith makes it *possible* for Him to do what He desires to do.

Faith is that unquestioning trust that caused Abraham to leave home, friends, property, security, to wander a lifetime and to die at last, still anticipating, but knowing God would not fail him.

Faith is that confidence that prompted boil-ridden Job, on his pile of ashes, reduced to penury, to exclaim, "Though he slay me, yet will I trust in him."

Faith is that trustful commitment to God that allowed

Peter to sleep soundly the night before he was supposed to be put to death.

But, you say, I have heard before the illustrations presented, or similar ones, and I know what they teach is true. But I still do not seem to have faith. As a result I am weak in spiritual power, my assurance of sins forgiven is a wavering one, I am unable to witness to a confidence in God, and I have no firm assurance of salvation.

The illustrations we started off with had to do with faith in people. Let's think in the same context in trying to find an answer to our problem. Let's ask, What reasons can we find for not having faith in a person? We think of two.

One Year Made the Difference

One, we are not going to trust a person with anything of importance unless we know enough about him to trust him. By way of example, suppose a total stranger knocks on my door one evening and asks to borrow $50. There is, I suppose, a slim possibility that his explanation would convince me I ought to loan him the money. But most likely I would decline his request. But one year later I might hand him the keys to my $3,000 car if he asked to borrow it, without a qualm. Why? Because in the interim I had gotten to know him so well I was confident I could trust him.

One reason why people do not have faith in God is because they have really gotten to know Him.

Ellen White has defined faith as "the clasping of the hand of Christ in every emergency" (*Gospel Workers,* p. 262). But you aren't going to trust yourself in any emergency to someone you do not know. Therefore, only getting to know God intimately will permit us to rest ourselves so confidently as is pictured here. We have discussed this subject in a previous chapter. (Of course, in discussing this facet of faith, we do not mean that only in emergencies do we go to God or exercise faith in Him.)

The second reason we may not have faith in a person is because he has failed us before. With men this has often happened; with God, never.

Speaking to Israel, both Joshua and Solomon stated that

not one word of all that God had promised had failed (Joshua 23:14; 1 Kings 8:56). At the end of a long and eventful life, Paul could write of God, "he abideth faithful" (2 Tim. 2:13), and "he is faithful that promised" (Heb. 10:23). Never, if we meet the conditions, will we be able to claim that God has failed us.

There are two other reasons we add for a person's failing to have faith in God. One is what the Bible terms "an evil heart of unbelief" (chap. 3:12). The term is used by Paul to describe the attitude of the Israelites in the wilderness, but it is still found today.

> Many look back to the Israelites, and marvel at their unbelief and murmuring, feeling that they themselves would not have been so ungrateful; but when their faith is tested, even by little trials, they manifest no more faith or patience than did ancient Israel. When brought into strait places, they murmur at the process by which God has chosen to purify them. Though their present needs are supplied, many are unwilling to trust God for the future. . . . Some are always anticipating evil, or magnifying the difficulties that really exist, so that their eyes are blinded to the many blessings which demand their gratitude. The obstacles they encounter, instead of leading them to seek help from God, the only Source of strength, separate them from Him, because they awaken unrest and repining. —*Patriarchs and Prophets*, pp. 293, 294.

Another reason we observe as a cause for the lack of faith in God is an unwillingness to meet the conditions laid down for receiving it, for faith is first a gift (Rom. 12:3; Heb. 12:2). These various conditions we have discussed in previous chapters.

Developing Faith

How do we develop faith? Well, how do we develop trust in a new friend? We listen to him talk and learn his philosophy of life, and his moral and ethical standards. We observe whether his actions line up with his profession. We listen to others' evaluation of him and their experience with him.

We usually do not set about, consciously, rationally, to evaluate a friend. It comes as a result of being together and seeing him under a variety of circumstances, and discussing a wide spectrum of subjects with him. We learn of his character, in other words, in the ordinary process of life.

Further, we get to know the genuineness, the dependability, the honesty, of a friend, by testing him. Again, we generally do not do this with planned deliberation. It usually happens casually, often haphazardly. But unless this process takes place we cannot really learn whether he is dependable, generous, sympathetic, helpful, and so on.

Nor do we stand much chance of learning what he is like unless we are involved in specifics with him. To illustrate: Suppose I am told a friend of mine is a good mechanic, which I am not. I begin to notice that my car is not acting as it should, so I say, "Bill, could you come over and take a look at my car one of these days? It doesn't seem to be working right." And he answers, "O.K. Any time."

I'll never really know whether he meant it or not, or whether he is a good mechanic or not, until I say, "Bill, I think my carburetor isn't working right. Could you help this afternoon?" And he says, "Sure, I'll be over at three o'clock."

When he turns up at three, and efficiently goes to work on my car, and gets it fixed, I am learning something about Bill. One thing I am learning is that I may have faith in him.

It is the same with God. We are frequently altogether too vague, too general, with Him. We say, "God, I'd like Your help." We make our requests so general that there is no way of discovering whether He grants them or not. And how can faith be developed under those conditions?

God is more interested in, and much more capable of, helping us than is a friend. He is eager to show His willingness to help. "Put me to the test, says the Lord of hosts" (Mal. 3:10, R.S.V.). It is true that, in context, Malachi is writing about tithes and offerings. But I am sure we can make an application in other areas. God doesn't promise to help and bless us only on the basis of our generosity with our checkbooks.

When we prove God, He helps; He is seen to be trustworthy. Our faith in Him grows.[54]

Recall the confident statement of Paul, after long years of serving Christ: I "am persuaded that he is able to keep that which I have committed unto him against that day" (2 Tim.

1:12). How so? "For I *know* whom I have believed."

Faith is closely connected with choice; with an act of the will. It sometimes requires deliberate effort of the will to expel doubt from the mind and to decide to believe God and to trust Him.

Confidence, No Matter What

We have learned what God is like through the revelation of His word. We have experienced the blessings, the peace, the joy, the freedom, that comes through Jesus. Now we must calculatedly place our confidence in Him, no matter what.

> At times . . . to exercise faith seems utterly contrary to all the evidences of sense or emotion; but our will must be kept on God's side. We must believe that in Jesus Christ is everlasting strength and efficiency.—*Our High Calling*, p. 124.
>
> There are those who find it hard to exercise faith, and they place themselves on the doubting side. These lose much because of their unbelief. If they would control their feelings, and refuse to allow doubt to bring a shadow over their own minds and the minds of others, how much happier and more helpful they would be.—*The SDA Bible Commentary*, Ellen G. White Comments, on Matt. 28:17, p. 1110.

We must, then, choose to trust God. Having established in our hearts and minds that He is true, we must place our minds in an attitude of trust toward Him. This advice is sound psychologically, as well as spiritually. John Wesley's Moravian friend, Peter Boehler, advised him, "Live by faith until you have faith."

Ellen White gives the same kind of advice:

> If you want faith, talk faith; talk hopefully, cheerfully.—*Testimonies*, vol. 1, p. 699.
>
> Those who talk faith and cultivate faith will have faith, but those who cherish and express doubts will have doubts.—*Ibid.*, vol. 5, p. 302.
>
> You have to talk faith, you have to live faith, you have to act faith, that you may have an increase of faith; and thus exercising that living faith you will grow to strong men and women in Christ Jesus.—*The SDA Bible Commentary*, Ellen G. White Comments, on Luke 17:5, pp. 1121, 1122.
>
> Faith is simple in its operation and powerful in its results. Many

professed Christians, who have a knowledge of the sacred Word, and believe its truth, fail in the childlike trust that is essential to the religion of Jesus. They do not reach out with that peculiar touch that brings the virtue of healing to the soul.—*Ibid.,* Ellen G. White Comments, on Rom. 5:1, p. 1074.

Ellen G. White gives two other requirements necessary for faith: "In order for a man's faith to be strong, he must be much with God in secret prayer."—*Testimonies,* vol. 4, p. 236. "In order to strengthen faith, we must often bring it in contact with the Word."—*Education,* p. 254.

We close with a word of caution, exhortation, and assurance. First, the words of caution and exhortation:

> If we sink down and give way to the temptations of Satan, we shall grow weaker and get no reward for the trial, and shall not be so well prepared for the next. In this way we shall grow weaker and weaker, until we are led captive by Satan at his will.—*Christian Experience and Teachings,* p. 103.
>
> The very time to exercise faith is when we feel destitute of the Spirit. When thick clouds of darkness seem to hover over the mind, then is the time to let living faith pierce the darkness and scatter the clouds.—*Ibid.,* p. 126.

Then there is this statement: "Faith grows by conflicts with doubts" *(Sons and Daughters of God,* p. 191).

Words of Assurance

The words of assurance are from *The Desire of Ages,* page 833. After her description of Jesus' ascension from the Mount of Olives, Ellen White tells of how the disciples went back to Jerusalem in gladness and triumph, full of praise and thanksgiving, their faces aglow with happiness. Then she writes:

> The disciples no longer had any distrust of the future. They knew that Jesus was in heaven, and that His sympathies were with them still. They knew that they had a friend at the throne of God, and they were eager to present their requests to the Father in the name of Jesus. In solemn awe they bowed in prayer, repeating the assurance, "Whatsoever ye shall ask the Father in my name, he will give it you. Hitherto have ye asked nothing in my name: ask, and ye shall receive, that your joy may be full." John 16:23, 24. They extended the hand of faith higher and higher, with the mighty argument, "It is Christ that died, yea rather, that is risen again,

who is even at the right hand of God, who also maketh intercession for us." Rom. 8:34.

The same assurance the disciples had, we may have. And we also may extend the hand of faith higher and ever higher, for we have a living, loving Saviour who can help us to overcome every sin, meet every emergency, do every task He lays upon us to do, and to stand at last, victorious before the throne.

A Question of Feelings

FEELINGS, by which we mean emotions, are a part of living. We are not dispassionate machines or soulless automatons. To various degrees and at various times we feel happy or sad, confident or anxious, disappointed or satisfied, angry or pleased. Situations and conditions about us—our own thinking, and the fluctuations of our biochemical make-up—engender certain feelings to which we respond to greater or lesser degrees. Our response depends upon how much self-control we have, on the conditions of our nerves at the time, on the habit patterns we have developed with respect to them, and so on.

Because feelings are so intimate, so very pervasive, so potentially preoccupative, so influential, over our thinking and our actions and reactions, the Christian wants to know what his attitude must be toward them.

Some people have stronger feelings than others. And some are directed by their feelings more than others. Often this is not so much because they have stronger feelings as that they have not learned to control them. A defendant on trial who pleaded with the judge that he had acted from "an uncontrollable impulse" was told by the judge that an uncontrollable impulse is simply an impulse uncontrolled.

There are, of course, two broad categories of feelings, good and bad. Even the good need to be controlled. For example, generosity is a good trait. But one may be generous to the point where he impoverishes his own family. In this chapter we are concerned with bad, undesirable feelings, from the perspective of Christian victory. For there are feelings that the worldling, and even the nominal Christian, would see absolutely no need, or no possibility, of overcoming, which the victorious Christian—by which I mean one who conquers every inherited and cultivated tendency to evil—will overcome in Jesus' strength.

Undesirable feelings (as well as desirable) spring from two sources or causes: personal or internal, and external. The personal may itself be separated into two categories: physical and emotional. The physical causes may be sickness, headaches, hunger, improper diet or overeating, lack of sleep, tiredness, or merely one of the many cycles the human body undergoes. The emotional may be, as an example, from a disturbed conscience with its accompanying sense of guilt.

External causes may include members of the family, friends, neighbors, or fellow workers. It may be occasioned by a job situation, finances, and many others.[55]

When We're Hungry We Eat

Dealing with the physical causes for undesirable feelings may be fairly simple. Generally, when hungry, we eat. Tiredness may be corrected by rest. (Ellen White warns against becoming overly tired, if it can be avoided. Because of our tendency to irritableness, et cetera, when we are tired, Satan can use it as a means of tempting us.)[56] A headache may be caused by the violation of some elementary law, and be quickly corrected.

Satan, who is always on the watch to catch us off guard and to attack at our weakest moments, will without doubt attack under these circumstances. He attacked Christ when the Saviour was weakened by forty days of fasting. But as He overcame, so may we overcome in His strength.

A guilty conscience is less simple to correct, often because we are not willing to take the steps necessary to make right the things that occasioned the feeling. A guilty conscience can find true relief only in Jesus.

> When guilt oppresses the soul and burdens the conscience, . . . remember that Christ's grace is sufficient to subdue sin and banish the darkness. Entering into communion with the Saviour, we enter the region of peace.—*The Ministry of Healing,* p. 250.

Sometimes equally difficult, sometimes more difficult, than getting rid of guilt, is dealing with problems we have with others. (Often, of course, they are tied together.) But we can always remember that if, having done all we can, we leave the matter in God's hands He will do the rest.

Depending on the situation, our undesirable feelings may be disappointment, depression, self-pity, hurt, resentment, irritability, impatience, jealousy, dislike, hostility, malice, envy, remorse, anxiety, or just plain moodiness. The name is legion. We may also remember that "many are unhappy because they are unholy" (ELLEN G. WHITE, in *Review and Herald,* June 30, 1891).

These feelings may result in a short temper, cynicism, gossip or backbiting, undermining another, uncooperativeness—the list is long. Worst of all, unhindered, they result in the death of any spiritual experience one may have; or in the withering of the developing one.

Dealing With Undesirable Emotions

How is the Christian to deal with those undesirable emotions, which he knows to be rooted in sin?

Can a person really control his reactions to his feelings? Moreover, can he eliminate the wrong feelings themselves? For every person desiring to be a Christian knows that, even though he may control his reactions to a sinful feeling, the feeling itself is spiritually defiling.

The answer to the first question is not difficult.

> Many who profess not the love of God do control their spirit to a considerable extent without the aid of the special grace of God. They cultivate self-control. This is a rebuke to those who know that from God they may obtain strength and grace, and yet do not exhibit the graces of the Spirit.—*Testimonies,* vol. 3, p. 336.

At one time I worked for a man who had one of the most even tempers I have ever witnessed. Many things happened on the job to fluster and upset him. But never once did I

7

see him manifest even the hint of irritation. On one occasion I remarked to him about his self-control, stating that I supposed he was naturally of a placid nature.

"I used to have a volcanic temper," he answered. "But I knew I had to overcome it, so I went to work on it with the help of Jesus." The result was apparent.[57]

> No one will enter the kingdom of God unless his passions are subdued, unless his will is brought into captivity to the will of Christ.—ELLEN G. WHITE, in *Review and Herald,* April 28, 1891.
>
> No impatient man or woman will ever enter into the courts of heaven. We must not allow the natural feelings to control our judgment. . . . Many who profess the truth, do not seem to realize that it is an essential part of religion to become meek and lowly, tenderhearted and forbearing.—*Ibid.,* Feb. 21, 1888.

There are some feelings that must be eliminated from the soul, because they are sinful. There are others that are not sinful, but the result of human weakness. They will dog the steps of the Christian until he puts off this vile body in exchange for a glorified one. Hatred, envy, self-pity, irritability, impatience, resentment, jealousy, malice, and all kindred feelings must be eradicated from the life. They are of the type Paul lists in Galatians 5:19-21. They are un-Christlike. They mar the character; and only the unmarred character will be admitted into the pure kingdom of our Lord. "Purity is demanded not only in the outward life but in the secret intents and emotions of the heart."—*Patriarchs and Prophets,* p. 308.

Emotions That Are Not Sinful

Discouragement, depression,[58] gloominess, and emotions of that order are emotions that must be decidedly and determinedly faced and conquered. They are not sinful in themselves. But they undermine faith, weaken resolution, and thus lead to sin.

> Your feelings might not always be of a joyous nature; clouds would at times shadow the horizon of your experience; but the Christian's hope does not rest upon the sandy foundation of feeling. Those who act from principle, will behold the glory of God beyond the shadows, and rest upon the sure word of promise. They will not be deterred from honoring God, however dark the way may seem.

Adversity and trial will only give them an opportunity to show the sincerity of their faith and love. When depression settles upon the soul, it is no evidence that God has changed. He is "the same yesterday, and to-day, and forever."—ELLEN G. WHITE, in *Review and Herald,* Jan. 24, 1888.

If you would know the mystery of godliness, you must follow the plain word of truth,—feeling or no feeling, emotion or no emotion. Obedience must be rendered from a sense of principle, and the right must be pursued under all circumstances. This is the character that is elected of God unto salvation.—*Ibid.,* July 17, 1888.

It is plain, then, that emotions are not to be consulted as a dependable barometer of our relationship with God. They are like the tides that rise and fall at the pull of sun and moon. Some incident, some remembrance, some word, some look, some bodily reaction, may raise your feelings to heights of joy or depths of gloom. In this connection Spurgeon said, "I looked to Jesus, and the dove of peace entered my heart. I looked at the dove, and it flew away." A Christian must not be a spiritual hypochondriac, watching every pulse of feeling.[59]

It is not your feelings, your emotions [good or bad], that make you a child of God, but the doing of God's will.—*Testimonies,* vol. 5, p. 515.

A pleasant, self-satisfied feeling is not an evidence of sanctification.—*The SDA Bible Commentary,* Ellen G. White Comments, on John 17:17, p. 1146.

In the heart of Christ, where reigned perfect harmony with God, there was perfect peace. He was never elated by applause, nor dejected by censure or disappointment. Amid the greatest opposition and the most cruel treatment, He was still of good courage.—*The Desire of Ages,* p. 330.

So it may be with us.

As we must not look to our feelings as the indicator of our relationship with God, so we must not talk of them to others. Expressing a feeling but confirms it, strengthens it, and makes it surer. To tell another that we are depressed, gloomy, disappointed, hurt, and so on, only makes it worse.

If you do not feel light-hearted and joyous, do not talk of your feelings. Cast no shadow upon the lives of others. A cold, sunless religion never draws souls to Christ. It drives them away from Him, into the nets that Satan has spread for the feet of the straying. Instead of thinking of your discouragements, think of the power you can claim in Christ's name. Let your imagination take hold upon things unseen. Let your thoughts be directed to the evidences of the great love of God for you.—*The Ministry of Healing,* p. 488.

When we talk discouragement and gloom, Satan listens with fiendish joy; for it pleases him to know that he has brought you into his bondage.—ELLEN G. WHITE, in *Review and Herald,* Feb. 27, 1913.

Feelings Fought, Fade

It is, then, the firm duty of every Christian troubled by feelings to resist decidedly every wrong and harmful emotion. This will often mean resisting the thought, the desire, the motivation, the attitude, behind the feeling. For example, moodiness may be caused by jealousy, envy, or thwarted ambition. Unless the cause is discovered, candidly admitted, and in the strength of Christ, repudiated, there is only a small gain in fighting the feeling itself. The root of bitterness must be destroyed. Feelings that are tackled in this way will gradually fade and be forgotten.

One final word of caution:

It is not wise to look to ourselves and study our emotions. If we do this, the enemy will present difficulties and temptations that weaken faith and destroy courage. Closely to study our emotions and give way to our feelings is to entertain doubt and entangle ourselves in perplexity. We are to look away from self to Jesus.—*The Ministry of Healing,* p. 249.

Is Your Soul Breathing Properly?

EVERY Christian knows that he should pray, but not every Christian seems to realize deeply enough how indispensably important prayer is for the spiritual life.[60] It has been said that prayer is the breath of the soul. I am not putting it too strongly when I state that just as physical breath is literally the difference between biological life and death, so prayer is literally the difference between spiritual life and death.

The born-again person who does not practically grasp this vital fact cannot be a confident, successful, victorious Christian. Moreover, he will not be a Christian, in the true sense of the word, for long. He cannot be.

Of course, failing to pray is not the only reason for spiritual death. Nevertheless, I re-emphasize, failure to pray will bring the end of the vital spiritual life as surely as failure to breathe will end the physical life.

Prayer is not termed the breath of the soul for nothing. There are significant parallels between breathing and praying.

On one occasion Jesus told His disciples a parable by which He taught them the lesson "that men ought always to pray, and not to faint" (Luke 18:1). He was talking, of course, of losing heart, becoming discouraged, which is one meaning of the term *faint*. When one fails to pray he loses heart.

101

The parallel is apparent, of course. One reason why a person faints physically is because of a lack of air. And the Christian "faints" spiritually because of a lack of the spiritual "oxygen" that comes through prayer.

In Ephesians, chapter six, verses 13-17, the apostle Paul metaphorically likens certain elements important to the Christian to parts of an armor such as was worn by soldiers of his day. The belt he likens to truth; the breastplate to righteousness; the sandals to the gospel, the message of peace; the shield he sees as comparable to faith; the helmet, to salvation; and the sword, to the Scriptures.

Extending Paul's Metaphor

Paul's metaphor does not extend to the next element he mentions. But if the figure we have been using had occurred to him, he might very well have used it.

"Pray at all times in the Spirit," he then exhorted the Christian warrior (verse 18, R.S.V.). Applying our figure of prayer as the breath of the soul, we recognize that the warrior in battle who, for some reason, does not breathe properly cannot fight well. His power of endurance is very limited; his strength is soon gone; he is easily overcome. "Apart from prayer," says Carl Henry, "all our virtues are placed in peril, for prayer sustains them in weakness and guards us from pride in their presence."—*Christian Personal Ethics*, p. 582.

Each of these ideas gives us some conception of how essential is prayer for the Christian.

The essential nature of prayer is underscored in another way as we continue to liken prayer to breathing. We may stress this importance by asking, How many times do we breathe in a day? Once? Twice? Three times? Four times? The implications of these questions are, of course, somewhat ridiculous.

"But," someone asks, "are you actually implying that we should pray as continuously as we breathe?"

What "Pray Constantly" Means

Well, what does Paul mean when he counsels, "Pray

constantly" (1 Thess. 5:17, R.S.V.)? We believe he means we must have a continuous attitude, an undiminished spirit, of prayer. When the mind is occupied with the affairs of life there is an almost unconscious praying going on, like the background music that is so pervasive in so many stores and business institutions today. And when the mind is not otherwise occupied, prayer surges to the foreground and becomes the conscious music of the soul.[61]

> While engaged in our daily work, we should lift the soul to heaven in prayer. These silent petitions rise like incense before the throne of grace; and the enemy is baffled. The Christian whose heart is thus stayed upon God cannot be overcome. No evil arts can destroy his peace. All the promises of God's word, all the power of divine grace, all the resources of Jehovah, are pledged to secure his deliverance. It was thus that Enoch walked with God. And God was with him, a present help in every time of need.—*Gospel Workers,* p. 254.

> We may commune with God in our hearts; we may walk in companionship with Christ. When engaged in our daily labor, we may breathe out our heart's desire, inaudible to any human ear; but that word cannot die away into silence, nor can it be lost. Nothing can drown the soul's desire. It rises above the din of the street, above the noise of machinery. It is God to whom we are speaking, and our prayer is heard.—*Ibid.,* p. 258.

Of course, even praying without ceasing can become a spiritually meaningless, routine ritual; a sort of religious talking to oneself. It can be as empty of spiritual content and vitality as is the endlessly turned prayer wheel of the Tibetan Buddhist. It may become a dead habit of praying to which God has quit listening long ago. For prayer is far, far more than words, even in the mind. Prayer is talking to God with the heart. Its source must be deep in the heart. It springs from an experience with God.

So far I have been considering mainly the importance of prayer. I have written primarily with the Christian in mind. Now I want to turn to the "how-to" of prayer, which will bring us to some problems that even the long-time Christian has to confront sometimes. At the same time I hope to make some suggestions for those who have seldom, perhaps never, prayed before but who wish now to get through to God.

An Obstacle to Prayer

Before I get into this we must be aware of one obstacle to prayer that, unless removed, will make useless all our efforts to pray meaningfully, successfully.

The psalmist put his finger on it: "If I had cherished iniquity in my heart, the Lord would not have listened" (Ps. 66:18, R.S.V.).

These words should be examined carefully. The psalmist did not write, "If I had been a *sinner,* the Lord would not have listened." The text says, If I had *cherished* sin. A person may have committed a half-dozen murders, robbed two dozen banks, committed adultery, homosexuality, lied ten thousand times. But if he comes in prayer to God in genuine repentance, with a broken heart, God will forgive.[62] "The sacrifices of God are a broken spirit: a broken and a contrite heart, O God, thou wilt not despise" (Ps. 51:17).

On the other hand, even though a person has had his name on the church books for decades, if he comes to God nurturing a spirit of resentment against a brother, he has disconnected the line between himself and God. The line can only be reconnected when he is willing to surrender his resentment.

Now, to the "how-to" of prayer. I shall discuss it in the context of private, personal prayer, on the knees in the bedroom, the study, or wherever we find seclusion with God. The "pray without ceasing" attitude and habit springs out of this time spent with Him.

Personally, when I can, I like to prepare my mind and heart for this special time of communion with God by reading something appropriate from the Bible or Spirit of Prophecy, and to meditate a little. In this way my thoughts and emotions are directed away from my job or other activities, and tuned to communicate with heaven. "The reading of the word of God prepares the mind for prayer."—*Review and Herald,* March 11, 1880.

"I Don't Feel Like Praying!"

But suppose I cannot get into the spirit of prayer. Does this mean that I decide, I'm not in the mood for prayer; I don't have the feeling for it? Or I'm not fit to pray, or I'm too much of a sinner or a hypocrite to pray; there's no use? So I do not pray.

How you feel, or what you are, is not the important point at all. The important point is Do you need to pray? Do you need God? Do you need help from God? In all honesty, your answer must be Yes.

Now read this:

> Our great need is our only claim on God's mercy.—*The Desire of Ages*, p. 317.
> We have nothing to recommend us to God; but the plea that we may urge now and ever is our utterly helpless condition that makes His redeeming power a necessity.—*Ibid.*

So your very condition of mind and heart is the very reason why you must pray.

Now, on your knees, begin to pray in a positive spirit of thankfulness. And don't try to tell yourself that you have nothing to be thankful for, that your whole roof has fallen in. Suppose it has. You are still alive. God is still there. He is good. He loves you. He is more than willing to listen to all your problems, and to help. And be thankful for prayer itself, which gives you a channel to God. Suppose you didn't have that?

But if you feel you can't be thankful—you might feel rebellious, instead—*pray!* Keep your need in the forefront—"God, this is the way I feel, but I need *You*. I need Your help, the kind only You can give."

Pray in the name of Jesus. He is the ordained Intermediary by which we approach the Father. "Whatsoever ye shall ask in my name," Jesus told His disciples, "that will I do" (John 14:13).

Pray in faith. But, you say, that's part of my problem; I don't seem to have faith. But the very fact that you are praying almost certainly indicates that you have some faith. You believe there is a God! You wouldn't try praying to "nobody or nothing." In that one belief, if in nothing else, you can exercise faith. Like the father of the demon-possessed boy who came in agony of spirit to Jesus to free his son, we may say, "Lord, I believe; help thou mine unbelief" (Mark 9:24).

105

> God will bestow upon us every needed blessing if we ask Him in simplicity and faith.—*Testimonies*, vol. 5, p. 201.
>
> It is a part of God's plan to grant us, in answer to the prayer of faith, that which He would not bestow did we not thus ask.— *The Great Controversy*, p. 525.
>
> Be earnest; be resolute. Present the promise of God, and then believe without a doubt. Do not wait to feel special emotions before you think the Lord answers. Do not mark out some particular way that the Lord must work for you before you believe you receive the things you ask of Him; but trust His word, and leave the whole matter in the hands of the Lord, with full faith that your prayer will be honored, and the answer will come at the very time and in the very way your heavenly Father sees is for your good; and then live out your prayers.—*Messages to Young People*, p. 123.

Ask for the presence of the Holy Spirit to soften and impress your heart. Ask Him to give you contrition and repentance as you need it; to help you to commit yourself sincerely to God.

Don't Quit

Don't, don't become discouraged and quit praying because nothing seems to happen the first time, or the first several times, you pray. Sometimes God has to set certain machinery in motion to answer our prayers, or it may take time for us to recognize that He really is at work for us.[63]

Sometimes God does not answer our prayers immediately so that we ourselves may be led to examine our faith, our sincerity, our real need of what we prayed for.

There is another reason:

> God does not always answer our prayers the first time we call upon Him; for should He do this, we might take it for granted that we had a right to all the blessings and favors He bestowed upon us. Instead of searching our hearts to see if any evil was entertained by us, and sin indulged, we would become careless, and fail to realize our dependence upon Him, and our need of His help.— ELLEN G. WHITE, in *Review and Herald*, June 9, 1891.

God's Wants Rather Than Ours

Pray according to God's will. It is easy to be self-centered and self-seeking in prayer. Sometimes we are so involved in thinking of what we want that we forget what God wants.

In our prayers we may ask for protection from certain

trials and dangers; we may ask to be kept from sickness, from the loss of property, or job, or friends. But God may know that just the thing we are asking to be saved from is the very experience we need to save our souls. So "Not my will, but Thine be done" must be the hub of every prayer. This means that each time we pray we will give our wills to His will. Prayers acceptable to God are unselfish prayers.

And in our praying we must put spiritual things first. "Seek ye first the kingdom of God . . ."

In all things, under all circumstances, pray. "It is impossible for the soul to flourish while prayer is neglected."—*Steps to Christ,* p. 98. "The darkness of the evil one encloses those who neglect to pray."—*Ibid.,* p. 94.

Let no feeling, no circumstance, no condition, no attitude, nothing, discourage you from prayer.⁵⁴ Prayer is the breath, the life line, of the soul. "Prayer is heaven's ordained means of success in the conflict with sin and the development of Christian character."—*The Acts of the Apostles,* p. 564.

The Fourth Japanese Monkey

WE HAVE all seen replicas of the little Japanese monkeys sitting in a row. The first has its paws over its eyes, signifying, See no evil. The second is covering its ears, denoting, Hear no evil. The third has its paws over its mouth, indicating, Speak no evil. The fourth—well, there isn't a fourth. But there ought to be! Someday some enterprising curio maker may add a fourth. It will be sitting beside the others with its paws over its forehead—Think no evil. And that will be the most important monkey of all.

For while it is essential that we see, hear, and speak no evil, evil itself has more to do with the mind than with the three faculties suggested by the curio. When we think no evil there is a good chance indeed that we can avoid seeing, hearing, and speaking evil.

The brain is the focus and center of our input and output. The eyes, ears, tongue, and other sensory organs are linked with the brain. The brain is the thought center. So what enters or leaves by the senses noted, and others, is connected with the mind and in some manner affects our thoughts.

A Link in Sin's Chain

Thought, then, is one of the links in the chain leading to sin. In his book *Let Me Assure You,* Edward W. H. Vick lists six steps leading from temptation to sin (pages 88-90).

108

The Fourth Japanese Monkey

The first is **attention.** "You see something, you hear something, you feel something, you think something" that tempts you to sin.

The second is **considering.** The first step, attention, is not sin. Sin may begin with the second link, consideration, or *thought*, about the matter that attracts attention.[65]

It depends on the way the mind deals with the sight, sound, feeling, or thought, that decides whether the individual goes through the remaining steps—**desire, decision, plan,** and **action.**

And, of course, one does not have to get all the way through the steps to action before he has sinned, as Vick points out. To permit the third step, wrong desire, to develop is sin—"If a man looks on a woman with a lustful eye, he has already committed adultery with her in his heart" (Matt. 5:28, N.E.B.).

Thus, the temptation must be nipped in the bud at its very inception in the mind if we are to prevent its becoming sin.[66]

It must not be entertained by the mind at all. Every suspicious-looking stimulus knocking at the mind's door must be met warily. And the instant it is recognized for what it is, a temptation to sin in any way, the door must be slammed in its face. There is no safety in being polite under the circumstances. Swift decision in the right direction is essential.

Expel Temptation Immediately

And if temptation arises, like a wraith, in the mind, it must instantly be expelled.[67] "Yielding to temptation begins in permitting the mind to waver, to be inconstant in your trust in God."—*Thoughts From the Mount of Blessing*, p. 92.

"By parleying with the enemy, we give him an advantage."—*The Desire of Ages*, p. 121. Satan is the master salesman. Once we give him the opportunity to begin his sales talk we are half sold already. It is always easier to get rid of a salesman outside your door. Once he is inside and begins his sales pitch the task is much more difficult.[68]

> The thoughts must be bound about, restricted, withdrawn from branching out and contemplating things that only weaken and defile the soul. The thoughts must be pure, the meditations of the heart must be clean.—*Review and Herald,* June 12, 1888.

It has never been easy for the Christian to distinguish all the deceptive subtleties of Satan and men. He has always needed a perception sharpened by the Holy Spirit to distinguish, in many cases. But the need for this sanctified keenness has never been greater than today, for a hundred insidious voices from within and without the church speak with "cunning craftiness."

One aspect of this craftiness is illustrated by the late C. S. Lewis in his interesting little book *The Screwtape Letters.* There he points out that not only does Satan endeavor to fill our minds with evil thoughts but he also works to keep good thoughts from occupying them. We are all aware of the first fact, but it is possible that the second scarcely, if ever, enters our minds; for his efforts to keep us from virtuous thoughts will patently have to be more subtle than his attempts to make us think evil ones. We generally have little trouble knowing when someone is trying to force a matter upon us. But we do not always catch on so quickly when the person furtively tries to steal something or keep something from us.

Not a Mental Vacuum

So, maintaining an unsullied mind requires more than merely expelling evil thoughts. For if that were possible the result would be merely a mental vacuum. Obviously, the positive act of thinking good thoughts is also essential. In fact, the thinking of good thoughts is about the only feasible way in which a person can exclude bad thoughts, for just as in the physical world no two material substances can occupy the same space at the same time, so also in the mental sphere no two thoughts can occupy the same mind at the same time.

This idea is implicit in Paul's familiar words of exhortation: "Finally, brethren, whatsoever things are true, whatsoever things are honest, whatsoever things are just, whatsoever things are pure, whatsoever things are lovely, whatsoever things are of good report; if there be any virtue, and if there be any praise, think on these things" (Phil. 4:8).

> If we would permit our minds to dwell more upon Christ and the heavenly world, we should find a powerful stimulus and support in fighting the battles of the Lord. Pride and love of the world will lose their power as we contemplate the glories of that better land so soon to be our home. Beside the loveliness of Christ, all earthly attractions will seem of little worth.—*Messages to Young People,* p. 113.

In these ideas we find one important reason why it is essential that we read and study our Bibles and the Spirit of Prophecy writings.

Mental discipline, such as is called for here, is not always easy. This is especially so if the thoughts have been permitted or encouraged for years to run in wrong channels, or simply to entertain any idea that happened along.[60]

> When the mind has been long permitted to dwell only on earthly things, it is a difficult matter to change the habits of thought. That which the eye sees and the ear hears too often attracts the attention and absorbs the interest.—*Ibid.*

But we need not struggle alone:

> If they [men and women] are weak in virtue and purity of thoughts and acts, they can obtain help from the Friend of the helpless. Jesus is acquainted with all the weaknesses of human nature, and, if entreated, will give strength to overcome the most powerful temptations. All can obtain this strength if they seek for it in humility.—*Child Guidance,* pp. 466, 467.

Excluding Even Good Things

There is another thought that needs to be considered: There are some subjects, good in themselves, that the Christian cannot take time to become involved with.

> We must turn away from a thousand topics that invite attention. There are matters that consume time and arouse inquiry, but end in nothing. The highest interests demand the close attention and energy that are so often given to comparatively insignificant things. —*The Ministry of Healing,* p. 456.

Life is short. Time is fleeting. Probation is brief. We have but a few years at most in which to perfect characters for eternity. Christ is coming. Our whole attention, all our efforts, must be governed by these thoughts. Ellen White says that we ought to live and act wholly with reference to the coming of the Son of man.

In our emphasis on mental discipline, there is one thought we must ever bear in mind.

> Christ alone can direct the thoughts aright. He alone can give noble aspirations, and fashion the character after the divine similitude. If we draw near to Him in earnest prayer, He will fill our hearts with high and holy purposes, and with deep longings for purity and righteousness.—*Counsels to Parents and Teachers,* p. 323.

Our major emphasis in this chapter has been on the need of closing the mind to every suggestion of evil. We also need to emphasize the importance of having a mind open to the truths of God found in the Bible and the Spirit of Prophecy writings.

In these sources we have truths upon which we can depend. We do not have to go to them as to other writings, with minds on guard to watch for possible error. In this respect we can relax.

Closed Minds, Open Minds

In fact, to the same degree that we should close our minds to all sinful thoughts, we should open them to the Bible and Spirit of Prophecy writings.

There will be times when we shall find, in our study of these books, ideas and requirements that will stir feelings of resistance in us.[70] Human nature, the carnal man, may and probably will at times rise up in rebellion against the counsels we find. The very fact that these feelings arise is a clue that we must surrender to Christ on that particular point. They are a signal that we need to search our hearts to understand why those emotions awoke. They are an indication that there are areas in our lives not yet fully conformed to the will of God. They are indicators that we would be wise not to ignore.

Two Fundamental Lessons

THE disciples looked at Christ in amazement, hardly able to believe that He had actually said what their ears heard.

A young man had just approached their Master with the question "Teacher, what good deed must I do that I may have eternal life?"

Jesus' first response was, "Keep the commandments." To make clear what He meant He mentioned several of the Ten Commandments.

"I have kept all of these," the young man said. "Where do I still fall short?"

Now, this young man happened to be very rich. Jesus knew that his riches were at the center of his life and that as long as this was so he could never enter into the kingdom of heaven. So He said, "If you want to be perfect, go and sell your property, and give the proceeds to the poor. Then you will have possessions in heaven."

For a moment the man weighed Jesus' statement; then, without a word, he turned away. The sacrifice was too great.

As Jesus looked after his retreating figure He said to the disciples, sadly, "It is easier for a camel to squeeze through the eye of a needle than for a rich man to get into heaven."

It was this statement that astounded the twelve, for they had been taught that riches were a sign of God's favor, and poverty, of His disfavor. If this young man, whose great riches seemed to point to favor with God, could not make it into the kingdom, who could, they reasoned.

"Who, then, can be saved?" they asked in astonishment.

Noting their amazement, Jesus said, "Humanly speaking, it is impossible that anyone can be saved, but with God all things are possible."

The Two Lessons

In Jesus' words are two fundamental lessons that all who would be Christians must learn.* Until we do we have not really grasped the ABC's of Christianity.

1. Of himself, man is able to do absolutely nothing to earn his salvation. His efforts to live a holy life are doomed to failure.

2. Through Jesus Christ, His merits and His strength, man can meet every requirement and perform every act necessary for holy living and for salvation.

Many sincere Christians live on the assumption that, at least in part, their salvation depends upon themselves alone. "Many have an idea that they must do some part of the work alone," writes Ellen G. White. "They have trusted in Christ for the forgiveness of sin, but now they seek by their own efforts to live aright."—*Steps to Christ*, p. 69. They depend on Sabbathkeeping, tithe-paying, health reform, honest living, faithful Ingathering, and other works to assure salvation.

It is natural to fall into this attitude. One of the hardest lessons for a person desiring to be a Christian to learn is that he cannot, by his own efforts, overcome sin, that God does not ask him to overcome sin by his own efforts, and that anything he does on his own to overcome sin brings him no merit with heaven.

The one who sincerely tries by his own efforts to overcome his sins is bound, sooner or later, to discover the impossibility of his task. Like Paul, he is eventually driven to the realization, "What I would, that do I not; but what I hate, that do I. . . . For the good that I would, I do not:

---

* For the basic idea presented in this chapter I am indebted to the book *Absolute Surrender*, by Andrew Murray.

but the evil which I would not, that I do" (Rom. 7:15-19).

The man who truly tries of himself to keep the law finds that it drives him with a demanding inflexibility that exhausts him. He discovers that the standard is too high for him. In striving to reach it, he falls back, spent and defeated. He finds himself to be a slave, a puppet, to his sinful habits. In his struggle to overcome, he may get to feel resentful toward God. Guiltily, he may think: God, I've repented of my sins and asked for forgiveness. I'm trying to do Your will. Lord, I keep on asking You to help me overcome my sins. But I keep on falling. Somehow, You don't seem to help me.

Meanwhile, his conscience is at him because of his failure. He is dogged with a sense of guilt, and haunted with a feeling of frustration.

It may take a person a long time to learn the lesson that he cannot possibly do God's will on his own. When he does, he may drift into one of two situations. He may become a "nominal Christian," living continually a defeated life, but thinking there is nothing better, that this is the lot of the Christian. Or he may come to the conclusion What's the use! There is nothing to all this about Christianity being able to give you victory over your sins and weaknesses, and to bring peace and happiness. I might as well forget it.

Both Lessons Must Be Learned

There are many striving Christians who learn the first of our two lessons—that man cannot live a holy life, and thus merit salvation, by his own efforts. There seem to be fewer who learn the second lesson, that, through Christ, the sanctified life, Christian victory, is abundantly possible, that "with God all things are possible."

It is necessary for the Christian to learn both lessons before he can truly understand the way of salvation. If he does not learn the first lesson, that he cannot through his own efforts obey God, he will go on trusting in his own works, his own righteousness, and be lost.

If he does not learn that he can have full victory through Jesus, he will go through life defeated, frustrated, faithless.

And because he is faithless he cannot receive salvation.

The fact that we learn these lessons with such difficulty sometimes leads us to an imbalance in our Christian beliefs. There may be a tendency to emphasize God's forgiveness, rather than His demand for perfect obedience; a leaning toward emphasizing the *imputed* righteousness of Christ, with a consequent de-emphasis of His *imparted* righteousness.[1] In other words, we may be inclined to overaccentuate the righteousness that is offered to the sinner freely, and almost forget about the emphasis the Bible and the Spirit of Prophecy place upon the quality character all must develop. We may place a lot of emphasis upon such statements as "When it is in the heart to obey God, when efforts are put forth to this end, Jesus accepts this disposition and effort as man's best service, and He makes up for the deficiency with His own divine merit."—*My Life Today*, p. 250.

This is a tremendous thought and offers great hope and encouragement for the born-again Christian. But it is *only* for the genuinely born-again person, as will be seen by reviewing points made in chapter eight, for example.

There is in the statement no assurance for those who are tempted to feel that it may be used as an excuse for habitual failing and failing. The words offer no security for one who thinks that, because he desires to do right, and is doing his best on his own, he need have no concern, even when he does sin.

For a proper understanding of such statements, other passages need to be placed with them. We would suggest, for example, a careful study of the chapter "Without a Wedding Garment" in the book *Christ's Object Lessons* (pp. 307-319).

A Character That All Must Possess

Let us note briefly a few quotations from this chapter:

> The wedding garment represents the *character which all must possess* who shall be accounted fit guests for the wedding.—Page 307. (Italics supplied.)

> Only the covering which Christ Himself has provided can make us meet to appear in God's presence. This covering, the robe of His own righteousness, Christ will put upon every repenting, believing soul.—Page 311.

> It is in this life that we are to put on the robe of Christ's righteousness.—Page 319.

Then Ellen White tells us what the wedding garment represents:

> By the wedding garment in the parable is represented the pure, spotless character which Christ's true followers will possess. To the church it is given "that she should be arrayed in fine linen, clean and white" (Rev. 19:8) "not having spot, or wrinkle, or any such thing" (Eph. 5:27). The fine linen, says the Scripture, "is the righteousness of saints."—Page 310.

Now, note particularly exactly what Mrs. White says the garment is:

> It is the righteousness of Christ, His own unblemished character, that through faith is *imparted* to all who receive Him as their personal Saviour.—*Ibid.* (Italics supplied.)

A study of Ellen White's interpretation of the term *wedding garment*, as listed in the *Index* to her writings, reveals that of the thirteen times listed in which she refers to it, most of them are ambiguous—they could be understood as meaning either imputed or imparted righteousness, or both. But when she does become more specific, in almost all cases she seems to suggest *imparted* righteousness. In the quotation above she is unequivocal.

We also note that she refers in this connection to Revelation 19:8 ("the fine linen is the righteousness of saints"). *The SDA Bible Commentary* comments on this passage: "[The Greek term used] applies particularly to the sanctified deeds of the Christian, his victorious life developed by the grace of the indwelling Christ."—Vol. 7, p. 872.

Consider again what we have read: All who have a part in the wedding supper must have the wedding garment. That garment represents the "pure, spotless character which Christ's true followers will possess." But the emphasis Ellen White makes is not Christ's righteousness IMPUTED to us, rather it is that it must be IMPARTED.*[72]

What does this mean?

---

* When this requirement is emphasized, the question is frequently raised: But what about the thief on the cross? What chance did he have for anything but *imputed* righteous-

> God calls upon us to reach the standard of perfection, and places before us the example of Christ's character. In His humanity, perfected by a life of constant resistance of evil, the Saviour showed that through co-operation with Divinity, human beings may in this life attain to perfection of character.—*The Acts of the Apostles,* p. 531.
>
> What Christ was in His perfect humanity, we must be; for we must form characters for eternity.—*Testimonies to Ministers,* p. 173.
>
> That perfection of character which the Lord requires is the fitting up of the whole being as a temple for the indwelling of the Holy Spirit. God will accept of nothing less than the service of the entire human organism. . . . God desires to prepare a people to stand before Him pure and holy, that He may introduce them into the society of heavenly angels.—*Our High Calling,* p. 265.

There are literally scores of Spirit of Prophecy statements, expressing the same idea, that might be quoted.

If, then, we must have more than God's forgiveness and the imputed righteousness of Jesus, there is one thing that Christians must have in the life. That is—victory.

As one woman said to me, "It is not enough to have Jesus' righteousness cover my imperfections. That is marvelous. I'm so grateful for His forgiveness. But I must have victory in my life. I can't go on living in frustrated defeat."

And victory we may have. The Bible and the Spirit of Prophecy make it amply plain that complete victory over every sin, every weakness, every inherited tendency to evil, is abundantly sure, *if we meet the conditions.*

"His divine power has granted to us all things that pertain to life and godliness, through the knowledge of him who called us to his own glory and excellence, by which he has granted to us his precious and very great promises, that through these you may escape from the corruption that is in the world because of passion, and become partakers of the

---

ness? But he will be saved, won't he?

The implication being, Is this matter of imparted righteousness that important?

It is to be remembered first, that total, unconditional surrender, which brings justification, pardon, the new birth, is required. This surrender the thief made. Second, the very act of surrender brings the Holy Spirit into the life, and, "the impartation of the Spirit is the impartation of the life of Christ" (*The Desire of Ages,* p. 805). Thus the character of Christ had been and was being imparted to the thief during the few hours he lived. Righteousness begins to be imparted the moment it is imputed.

For a discussion of imparted in what is thought of as the "absolute" sense, see the two following chapters.

divine nature" (2 Peter 1:3, 4, R.S.V.).

"But thanks be to God, who in Christ always leads us in triumph" (2 Cor. 2:14, R.S.V.).

"But thanks be to God, who gives us the victory through our Lord Jesus Christ" (1 Cor. 15:57, R.S.V.).

"In all these things we are more than conquerors through him who loved us" (Rom. 8:37, R.S.V.).

"Sin will have no dominion over you, since you are not under law but under grace" (chap. 6:14, R.S.V.).

"I can do all things in him who strengthens me" (Phil. 4:13, R.S.V.).

"Now to him who is able to keep you from falling and to present you without blemish before the presence of his glory with rejoicing" (Jude 24, R.S.V.).

The following statements are representative of many found in the writings of Ellen G. White:

> Man is, through faith, to be a partaker in the divine nature, and to overcome every temptation wherewith he is beset.—*Our High Calling*, p. 48.
>
> We can overcome. Yes, fully, entirely. Jesus died to make a way of escape for us, that we might overcome every evil temper, every sin, every temptation, and sit down at last with Him.—*Testimonies*, vol. 1, p. 144.
>
> If we will trust Him, and commit our ways to Him, He will direct our steps in the very path that will result in our obtaining the victory over every evil passion, and every trait of character that is unlike the character of our divine Pattern.—*Our High Calling*, p. 316.
>
> Man may become a partaker of the divine nature; not a soul lives who may not summon the aid of Heaven in temptation and trial. Christ came to reveal the source of His power, that man might never rely on his unaided human capabilities.—*Selected Messages*, book 1, pp. 408, 409.
>
> The life that Christ lived in this world, men and women can live through His power and under His instruction. In their conflict with Satan, they may have all the help that He had. They may be more than conquerors through Him who loved them and gave Himself for them.—*Testimonies*, vol. 9, p. 22.

We shall return to this subject of victory in chapter 19, following the examination of other matters in the next three chapters.

Was Sataq Right?

"THERE lived in the land of Uz a man of blameless and upright life named Job, who feared God and set his face against wrongdoing" (Job 1:1, N.E.B.).

Around this man, Job, was enacted a drama that has intrigued and instructed men ever since. It is possible that Job himself never did learn of the unseen drama played behind the scenes, one that involved the great antagonistic powers in the universe, God and Satan.

The stage for the drama was set during a council, possibly of the rulers of the millions of inhabited worlds throughout the universe. Satan apparently attended as the prince of this world. A discussion is recorded between Jehovah and Satan, during which the latter suggests that the whole earth is under his control. God then reminds Satan that there is at least one man, Job, who is not his servant, but who obeys God.

At this Satan responds, " 'Has not Job good reason to be God-fearing [a term denoting loyalty and obedience to God]? Have you not hedged him round on every side with your protection, him and his family and all his possessions? . . . But stretch out your hand and touch all that he has, and then he will curse you to your face' " (verses 9-11).

The development and end of the drama, we all know. Although Satan was permitted to try Job to the limit, Job persevered in his faithfulness to God.

Satan's Perennial Challenge

The challenge that Satan threw down to God respecting Job's loyalty is one that he has been hurling through the centuries. It is one that involves every professed child of God. For, in essence, Satan was implying, "Look, Job really can't keep Your commandments. The only reason he seems to is because You are pampering and protecting him. But let him really be tested and You will find him too weak, too self-centered, to remain loyal. And every other human being is just like him."

> Satan represents God's law of love as a law of selfishness. He declares that it is impossible for us to obey its precepts.—*The Desire of Ages,* p. 24.
>
> From the very beginning of the great controversy in heaven, it has been Satan's purpose to overthrow the law of God. It was to accomplish this that he entered upon his rebellion against the Creator, and though he was cast out of heaven he has continued the same warfare upon the earth.—*The Great Controversy,* p. 582. (Cf. *The Desire of Ages,* pp. 29, 309, 761; *Patriarchs and Prophets,* p. 77.)

In *The Desire of Ages,* Ellen White describes the Jewish leaders of Jesus' day as echoing Satan's claim: "The rabbis virtually represented God as giving laws which it was impossible for man to obey" (page 284). Through the centuries, in one way or another, many religious leaders and followers have agreed with them.

But God claims that man can keep His law, and He expects him to do so. "May God himself, the God of peace, make you holy in every part, and keep you sound in spirit, soul, and body, without fault when our Lord Jesus Christ comes. He who calls you is to be trusted; he will do it" (1 Thess. 5:23, 24, N.E.B.). "If you give fortitude full play you will go on to complete a balanced character that will fall short in nothing" (James 1:4, N.E.B.). "Now unto him that is able to keep you from falling, and to present you faultless before the presence of his glory with exceeding joy" (Jude 24).

Many conservative theologians recognize the heights of accomplishment God requires of His people.

> In the New Testament the only Christian life *allowable* is that

of entire sanctification. For those who are stopping short of this there are exhortations, warnings, expostulations, invitations, prayers; but the life there presented to every believer is one of a surrendered will, an obedient heart, a victorious Spirit-filled life in union with Christ, bringing salvation from sin, and leading to steady growth, through increasing knowledge and manifold temptations.—JAMES HASTINGS, *Thessalonians to Hebrews,* p. 52.

After examining a number of Scripture words that describe God's moral requirements for His followers, R. B. Girdlestone comments:

It will thus be seen that the standard of perfection set before all Christians in the N.T. is very high indeed, no room being left for any wrong-doing; but the promise of needful power is equally explicit.—*Synonyms of the Old Testament,* p. 99.

Ellen G. White is direct and explicit in her statements regarding God's standard for His people:

Exact obedience is required, and those who say it is not possible to live a perfect life throw upon God the imputation of injustice and untruth.—In the *Review and Herald,* Feb. 7, 1957.

God requires at this moment just what He required of Adam in Paradise before he fell—perfect obedience to His law.—*Review and Herald,* July 15, 1890.

The obedience that Christ rendered God requires from human beings today.—*Christ's Object Lessons,* p. 282.

At this point we come to a problem that some Seventh-day Adventists have. Probably none of us have a problem concerning the eternal, unchangeable nature of God's law. We know that Jesus kept the law perfectly. We rightly believe that when we truly accept Him as our Saviour His unflawed obedience to the law is imputed to us so that we stand before God as if we had never sinned.

An Incredible Suggestion!

But some of us think the suggestion incredible, inconceivable, that we are expected to keep the law as perfectly as Jesus did. It is insisted by some that it is not possible for any man perfectly to meet that standard. Indeed, the Christian *is* bound to battle with sin throughout his life. But, it is implied, he is also bound to keep on failing, even if to a lesser and lesser degree. But by the very nature of the situation, it is suggested, he will keep on failing until Jesus returns. He can do nothing else because he was "shapen in iniquity; and in sin did . . . [his] mother conceive . . . [him]" (Ps. 51:5), while Jesus was born without any tendency to sin.

But one thought must overshadow all such concepts. If it is impossible for man, in the strength of Christ, to keep God's law perfectly, *then Satan is right; God is unfair.* It *is* impossible for us to obey the precepts of the law. God *is* asking too much of us.

There is another, even more crucial and important issue involved, even the honor of God Himself. Ellen G. White puts it this way:

> The Lord desires through His people to answer Satan's charges by showing the results of obedience to right principles.—*Christ's Object Lessons,* p. 296.
> The very image of God is to be reproduced in humanity. The honor of God, the honor of Christ, is involved in the perfection of the character of His people.—*The Desire of Ages,* p. 671.

Taking Another Look

The two concepts we have just considered—that if God cannot empower men to keep His law perfectly, Satan is right, and that the honor of God and the Son is bound up with our developing Christlike characters—demand that we take another look at our relationship to Christ, God, and the moral law.

Christ "emptied himself, taking the form of a servant, being born in the likeness of men. And being found in human form he humbled himself and became obedient unto death, even death on a cross" (Phil. 2:7, 8, R.S.V.). The Father sent "his own Son in a form like that of our own sinful nature" (Rom. 8:3, N.E.B.). "Therefore he had to be made like his brethren in every respect, so that he might become a merciful and faithful high priest" (Heb. 2:17, R.S.V.).

> Our Saviour took humanity, with all its liabilities. He took the nature of man, with the possibility of yielding to temptation. We have nothing to bear which He has not endured.—*Ibid.,* p. 117.
> Christ's overcoming and obedience is that of a true human being. . . .

> The obedience of Christ to His Father was the same obedience that is required of man. . . . He came not to our world to give the obedience of a lesser God to a greater, but as a man to obey God's Holy Law, and in this way He is our example.—*Our High Calling,* p. 48.

God's requirement for us, then, is to live the kind of perfect life men may live in their sphere.[73] It was that kind of life Christ lived, the life of the perfect man, not of a God. And—

> our work is to strive to attain in our sphere of action the perfection that Christ in His life on the earth attained in every phase of character. He is our example.—*That I May Know Him,* p. 130.
>
> The Lord requires perfection from His redeemed family. He expects from us the perfection which Christ revealed in His humanity. —*Child Guidance,* p. 477.

A Troubling Concept

At this point we are confronted with a subject that has challenged and troubled the Christian church for centuries and that challenges the Seventh-day Adventist Church today —that of perfection.

When we study the Spirit of Prophecy in the light of what God expects of His people, it is impossible to avoid the term, for Ellen White uses it over and over again in this connection. Because she uses it so often, and often places it in a context that helps us to understand what she means, we believe it is possible for us to get from her writings an understanding of the concept that builds on the Bible teaching, and that goes on to give us a magnified picture of the concept.

To understand the concept we need first to take a look at the term as used in the Bible.

This present book is not the kind of work in which the author goes into a detailed, scholarly examination of the Biblical terms, Hebrew and Greek, that are translated "perfect." A brief summary must suffice.

It is possible to explain the Hebrew words by observing that they mean, variously, among other definitions, complete, whole, entire, blameless, finished. But because the subject of perfection comes much more to the fore in the New Testament, it might be well to look a little more closely at the

Greek words there translated by various forms of the term "perfect"—the word, *teleios*. It comes from the root, *telos,* meaning, an end.

Teleios means, among other definitions, whole, perfect, full grown, fulfilled, mature, complete.

In his *Word Pictures in the New Testament,* A. T. Robertson comments on Matthew 5:48: "Be ye therefore perfect, even as your Father which is in heaven is perfect." "The word [perfect] comes from *telos,* end, goal, limit. Here it is the goal set before us, the absolute standard of our heavenly Father. The word is used also for relative perfection as of adults compared with children."

Of this text Ellen White says:

> God's ideal for His children is higher than the highest human thought can reach. "Be ye therefore perfect, even as your Father which is in heaven is perfect." This command is a promise. The plan of redemption contemplates our complete recovery from the power of Satan. Christ always separates the contrite soul from sin. He came to destroy the works of the devil, and He has made provision that the Holy Spirit shall be imparted to every repentant soul, to keep him from sinning.—*The Desire of Ages,* p. 311.

Perfect in Our Sphere

In *My Life Today,* page 38, Ellen White enlarges somewhat on Matthew 5:48 by writing, "We may be perfect in our sphere, even as God is perfect in His." We shall deal with this idea again in the following chapter.

Commenting on the noun form of the word, *telos,* which is *teleioi,* the perfect ones, Richard C. Trench observes:

> In a natural sense the τέλειοι [teleioi] are the adults, who, having attained the full limits of stature, strength, and mental power within their reach, have in these respects attained their τελος [telos], as distinguished from the νέοι [neoi] or παῖδες [paides], young men or boys.—*Synonyms of the New Testament,* p. 75.

Later, he summarizes:

> The distinction then is plain. . . . The τέλειος [teleios] is one who has attained his moral *end,* that for which he was intended, namely, to be a man in Christ; however it may be true that, having reached this, other and higher ends will open out before him, to have Christ formed in him more and more.—*Page* 77.

Truth Versus Fanaticism

Now, the fact that the idea of perfection has in the past led some men and women to make exaggerated, fanatical claims, and to practice fanatical, even immoral, acts, should not lead Seventh-day Adventists to repudiate the whole concept out of hand.[74] Exaggeration and fanaticism have been attached to many another Bible teaching, as well, but we don't reject these teachings because of that.

Moreover, the fact that Ellen White does not avoid or depreciate the concept, except when she is discussing fanaticism, but rather uses the term in a sense that often seems to approach the absolute meaning—by which I mean total and uninterrupted victory over every sin of thought, motive, and action that were in the life—should cause us to examine the idea carefully.

We believe that, on the basis of the Spirit of Prophecy writings, there is a way to understand the concept of perfection that will, in the main, eliminate the objections that have been raised against it over the centuries. This way is the subject of the following chapter.

Proving Satan Wrong

THE life of the born-again person is a life totally surrendered to Christ. This surrender is of the mind, heart, and will. The desires, the will, the motives, the ambitions, the attitudes, are now Christ-centered and Christ-directed rather than being self-centered and self-directed.

But while there is a "new heart," as just defined, this does not mean that every undesirable habit that has been deeply registered upon our brain and nerve cells is wiped out.[75] Those habit patterns are still there. They have to be repudiated, stiffly fought, conquered, kept under control, eliminated by us, with the help of Christ.

> The work of salvation is not child's play, to be taken hold of at will and let alone at pleasure. It is the steady purpose, the untiring effort, that will gain the victory at last. It is who endureth to the end that shall be saved.—*Testimonies,* vol. 2, pp. 101, 102.

> Those who would overcome must put to the tax every power of their being. They must agonize on their knees before God for divine power. . . . Divinity and humanity may be combined in them.—*The SDA Bible Commentary,* Ellen G. White Comments, on Matt. 4:1-11, p. 1082.

As day by day the continuously surrendered Christian cooperates with Christ in ridding himself of sinful propensities, his impulses to sin become weaker and weaker, and thus easier and easier to overcome. The sin pattern imprinted upon the brain cells where the habit is registered, becomes

---

weaker and weaker as it is gradually eliminated and replaced by the good habit impulse the Christian is developing.

> As we partake of the divine nature, hereditary and cultivated tendencies to wrong are cut away from the character, and we are made a living power for good. Ever learning of the divine Teacher, daily partaking of His nature, we co-operate with God in overcoming Satan's temptations. God works, and man works, that man may be one with Christ as Christ is one with God. Then we sit together with Christ in heavenly places. The mind rests with peace and assurance in Jesus.—ELLEN G. WHITE, in *Review and Herald,* April 24, 1900.

As day by day the Christian cooperates in the work of overcoming, the time comes when every impulse to sin has been subdued so that its impression upon the brain and nerve cells is too weak to trigger a reaction.

It is, I believe, of this condition that Ellen White writes:

> If we consent, He will so identify Himself with our thoughts and aims, so blend our hearts and minds into conformity to His will, that *when obeying Him we shall be but carrying out our own impulses.—The Desire of Ages,* p. 68. (Italics supplied.)

Does this mean that the Christian can get to the place where he will not sin?

> God calls upon us to reach the standard of perfection and places before us the example of Christ's character. In His humanity, perfected by a life of constant resistance to evil, the Saviour showed that through co-operation with Divinity, human beings may in this life attain to perfection of character. This is God's assurance to us that we, too, may obtain complete victory.—*The Acts of the Apostles,* p. 531.

> Exact obedience is required, and those who say that it is not possible to live a perfect life throw upon God the imputation of injustice and untruth.—ELLEN G. WHITE, in *Review and Herald,* Feb. 7, 1957.

> He who has not sufficient faith in Christ to believe that He can keep him from sinning, has not the faith that will give him an entrance into the kingdom of God.—ELLEN G. WHITE, in *Review and Herald,* March 10, 1904.

Objections to Perfection

There are, understandably, a number of objections that have been raised to the teaching of perfection because of past experiences, already alluded to. But perfection, as we believe it may be understood from the Spirit of Prophecy writings—

Does not mean holy flesh. "While we cannot claim perfection of the flesh, we may have Christian perfection of the soul."—*Selected Messages,* book 2, p. 32.

It does not mean that it is impossible to sin. This has been lucidly explained by someone who said, "It is not impossible to sin, but it is possible not to sin." "Christ came to this world and lived the law of God, that man might have perfect mastery over the natural inclinations which corrupt the soul."—*The Ministry of Healing,* pp. 130, 131.

It does not mean ever reaching a time when we will be able to make it on our own. "We cannot for one moment separate ourselves from Christ with safety."—*Messages to Young People,* p. 115. "Divine grace is needed at the beginning, divine grace at every step of advance, and divine grace alone can complete the work."—*Testimonies to Ministers,* p. 508.[76]

It does not lead one ever to feel that he is holy, perfect, or to have pride or self-confidence. One reason for this is that he who reaches the condition described by Ellen White will not know that he has.[77] This was apparently the case with Paul. During his first imprisonment in Rome he wrote his Epistle to the Philippians, in which he stated: "Not as though I had already attained, either were already perfect: but I follow after . . ." (Phil. 3:12). These words were written toward the end of the apostle's life; he was beheaded only about five years later. Yet of Paul, Ellen White wrote, "Paul attained to the full moral stature of a man in Christ Jesus."—*The SDA Bible Commentary,* Ellen G. White Comments, on Phil. 1:21, p. 903.

(We need to place beside the text just quoted, verse 15, in which Paul classes himself with those that are "perfect." This contradiction is only apparent, not real. The *SDA Bible Commentary,* in its comments on verse 15, says: "The concept here expressed does not conflict with the statement of Philippians 3:12, where Paul denies that he has reached the ultimate in perfection. Here [in verse 15] he is employing perfect in a relative sense.")

In the *Signs of the Times,* August 22, 1911, Mrs. White

9   129

stated, "You may not realize that you are growing up into Christ, your living Head. Your part is simply to submit your ways and your will to God. You are to trust yourself fully to God, knowing you cannot make yourself grow."

In this last phrase is found the main reason why he who reflects the character of Christ fully, even should he know that he does, will never feel that he has done the attaining, or will in any way be inclined to pat himself on the back. Humbly, he will know, through bitter experience, that he himself cannot get rid of his inherited and cultivated bent to sin. He has learned that his only strength, his only hope, his only sufficiency, his only possibility, is in his Saviour, who only can bring a good thing out of an evil thing.[78]

Because he who reaches the stage where he no longer commits sin, will not know it, and because "It is not impossible to sin, but it is possible not to sin," "we cannot say, 'I am sinless,' till this vile body is changed and fashioned like unto His glorious body."—ELLEN G. WHITE, in *Signs of the Times,* March 23, 1888.

Contradictory as it may at first thought seem to some, "in this life [to] attain to perfection of character" does not mean to become as unsurpassably perfect as God is perfect. It does not mean that one has reached the absolute, ultimate limits of growth. We have noted that Christians are to manifest the kind of perfect life *Jesus lived on earth.* Those who finally reach that condition will have, in cooperation with Him, done so from two aspects. They will have completely overcome the *negative* qualities in their lives, sin. And they will have added *positive* qualities. In other words, they will stop sinning, entirely, and will manifest fully in their present state the qualities of moral perfection shown by Christ *as a man.* Thus they will be perfect *in their sphere* as God is perfect in His, which is infinitely above man's.

As a man, Christ revealed a severely limited picture of His divinity. His glory, His character, was lived within boundaries to which human beings are limited. But, under those limitations, and revealing to man as much as man could grasp, Christ lived a perfect life, a fulfillment of the absolute idea of manhood.

Right here I wish to detour for a moment to bring in an idea that, while not directly connected with what we have been discussing, is nevertheless vitally related, and is very important in the context of our chapter title, "Proving Satan Wrong."

In *The Desire of Ages,* page 763, we read of the time when, from the viewpoint of the development of man's character, the controversy will have reached its peak. Referring to "the end of time," the author says:

> There will be but two classes. Every character will be fully developed; and all will show whether they have chosen the side of loyalty or that of rebellion.
> Then the end will come. God will vindicate His law and deliver His people.

Man's Blunted Faculties

Man, in the flesh, with all of his faculties vastly blunted by sin, is intellectually, spiritually, socially, esthetically, and sensorially limited. But all of this will be changed when the redeemed are given bodies "like unto his glorious body" (Phil. 3:21). With the sin principle, the negative element, entirely eliminated from the character, with minds and bodies infinitely better and more sensitive than those we now possess, we will begin growth of which we can now have no idea.[79] In Christ's kingdom—

> Every faculty will be developed, every capacity increased. The acquirement of knowledge will not weary the mind or exhaust the energies. There the grandest enterprises may be carried forward, the loftiest aspirations reached, the highest ambitions realized; and still there will arise new heights to surmount, new wonders to admire, new truths to comprehend, fresh objects to call forth the powers of mind and soul and body.—*The Great Controversy,* p. 677.
> And the years of eternity, as they roll, will bring richer and still more glorious revelations of God and of Christ. As knowledge is progressive, so will love, reverence, and happiness increase.—*Ibid.,* p. 678.
> Those who are under the instruction of Christ in this world will take every divine attainment with them to the heavenly mansions. And in heaven we are continually to improve.—*Christ's Object Lessons,* p. 332.

Thus, in this life, he who surrenders himself totally, unreservedly, to God will, in cooperation with Jesus, grow away from sin, the negative quality of life, until Jesus can "keep him from sinning." At the same time he will begin to grow in all the positive qualities—love, gratitude, appreciation, service, and others.[50] And he will continue to grow throughout eternity. In this, so far as man is concerned, there seems to be no absolute, no arriving, for these qualities are God's infinitely, and man will never be equal to Him.

It is essential that one further, very important, idea be added here. Because a Christian has so placed himself in the hands of Jesus, and his life has been so molded that he finally no longer commits sin, does not mean that he cannot sin. We previously quoted, "It is not impossible to sin, but it is possible not to sin." Let us examine the subject in the light of this statement.

There are quotations in the Spirit of Prophecy that, if not properly understood, seem to contradict what we have written. Portions of the following are among them:

> Sanctification is not the work of a moment, an hour, a day, but of a lifetime. It is not gained by a happy flight of feeling, but is the result of constantly dying to sin, and constantly living for Christ. . . . It is only by long, persevering effort, sore discipline, and stern conflict, that we shall overcome. . . . *So long as Satan reigns, we shall have self to subdue, besetting sins to overcome; so long as life shall last, there will be no stopping place,* no point which we can reach and say, I have fully attained. *Sanctification is the result of a lifelong obedience.—The Acts of the Apostles,* pp. 560, 561. (Italics supplied.)

A question that may be raised is this: If it is possible "in this life [to] attain to perfection of character;" if it is possible that Christ can "keep him [a Christian] from sinning," how is it that we are told that "so long as Satan reigns [which will be till the coming of Christ] we shall have self to subdue," and that "there will be no stopping place"?

An Allegory

Perhaps a simple allegory will help us to find a solution.

There is an island kingdom, with a fortified city as its headquarters, that has a tyrant as king.

There comes a time when the subjects of this kingdom

begin to groan under his tyranny, and wish to be rid of him. They put forth every effort to dethrone him, but to no avail. He is too strong, too entrenched, for them.

Finally they conclude, There is no use in our trying to depose the king. He has forces available that we do not have. The only way we shall be able to rid ourselves of him is by calling on another king to help us.

So they approach the king of another country and ask him to liberate them from the tyrant. He says, I will send my son, the crown prince, to aid you.

The prince agrees to help. But there are conditions. He says, "There is only one way I can help you. Your ruler is so strong, so subtle, so pervasive, that in order for me to defeat him you must give me absolute control, and do completely everything I ask of you."

They agree. Then he adds, "While I ask total cooperation and obedience if I am to be your king, I will rule you only as long as you want me to. I want to be wanted as your king. When you ask me to abdicate, I shall do so."

With this understanding the prince deposes the tyrant, and becomes the new king, ruling in love and benevolence.

But the tyrant, while he is no longer ruler, is still alive. He flees with his followers to some wild, barren mountains to the north of the island kingdom. From there, year after year, he carries on guerrilla warfare against the people and the city. And the subjects of the kingdom must be on constant, and vigilant, guard against him, and must ever look to their new king for aid.

Sometimes the old ruler, who is well acquainted with the weaknesses of his former capital, makes a sudden sally, and the city's defenses are momentarily breached. Sometimes the city's inhabitants relax their vigilance, and he takes them by surprise, overcoming them.[51] But immediately they call upon their new king, and he comes to their aid.

As long as the subjects of that kingdom are submitted to their new king, they can, with his help, turn these setbacks into victories, and thus they grow stronger day by day. At the same time the tyrant, in his barren mountains, is growing weaker and weaker.

As time goes on, the weakened former ruler loses every fight. He is constantly subdued, and never again successful in any raid he makes.[82]

But he is still alive and alert, always looking for an opportunity to defeat his former subjects, always harassing them, always making it essential that they never let down their guard, and that they look constantly to their new ruler for aid.

The Interpretation

The interpretation of the allegory is this:

The tyrant king is Sinful Self who is the natural ruler at the center of all men's lives. There are some men who, becoming unhappy with their ruler, decide they must get him out of their lives. So they put forth every effort to subdue him and his followers—various evil habits and tendencies, such as temper, appetite, malice, lust, envy, and so on. But they soon discover their inability to overcome. They then call upon God and He sends His Son, Jesus, to the rescue.

> [But] Christ asks for an unreserved consecration, for undivided service. He demands the heart, the mind, the soul, the strength. Self is not to be cherished. He who lives to himself is not a Christian. —*Christ's Object Lessons,* pp. 48, 49.

While Christ demands complete consecration, He will not demand it unwillingly. If we decide to permit self to assume control again, He will sorrowfully acquiesce to our wishes.

But once the surrender is made, Christ aids the sinner to expel self from the throne of the soul. But self is not destroyed by that act. He is still lurking in the life, waiting to manifest himself at any moment.[83]

> Self is difficult to conquer. Human depravity in every form is not easily brought into subjection to the Spirit of Christ. But all should be impressed with the fact that unless this victory is gained through Christ, there is no hope for them. The victory can be gained; for nothing is impossible with God. By His assisting grace, all evil temper, all human depravity, may be overcome.—*Testimonies,* vol. 4, p. 349.

Self can be conquered. The sinful human nature can be subdued, totally, through Christ.

> By resolute self-denial, by constant watchfulness, by earnest prayer, by the diligent use of every means of grace, and by the help

of Jesus Christ our Redeemer, we shall come off victorious.—*Our High Calling*, p. 82.

But self, subdued though it may be for years, is always there, potentially ready to take over the life. And it is not until Christ comes, and we are changed, that Sinful Self will finally be destroyed.

Proving Satan a Liar

Thus, I believe that the perfection Christ desires, and that Ellen White describes, is that full giving over of the life to Jesus that He may develop mature, complete, blameless, finished characters that will reflect fully the life He lived on earth, in which sinning had no part. The people who thus cooperate with Him will prove that, by His indwelling Spirit, His law can be fully kept. They will prove that Satan is a liar.

Some hold that the subject of perfection is not one upon which the Christian needs to dwell. While we do not believe the danger inherent in the usual understanding of the subject is found in the explanation we have given, still we would agree, except for one reason:

There is a great, overshadowing cause for the Christian to aspire, with the concentrated powers of his being, to the life that perfectly reflects the life of Jesus. It is because his greatest desire will be to vindicate the honor of his Lord and Saviour. He will want to prove to all the universe, to Satan and all his hosts, that the adversary is a liar, and that God is right.

Christ is asking this vindication of His remnant church in this generation. And this means you and me. For with this church as the nucleus, there will emerge the 144,000 who will fully cooperate with Him (see Rev. 18:4, 5).

> The church is the depositary of the wealth of the riches of the grace of Christ, and *through the church eventually will be made manifest the final and full display of the love of God to the world* that is to be lightened with its glory. The prayer of Christ that His church may be one as He was one with His Father, will finally be answered. The rich dowry of the Holy Spirit will be given, and through its constant supply to the people of God they will become witnesses in the world of the power of God unto salvation.—*Testimonies to Ministers*, p. 50. (Italics supplied.)
>
> Christ is waiting with longing desire for the manifestation of

Himself in His church. When the character of Christ shall be perfectly reproduced in His people, then He will come to claim them as His own.—*Christ's Object Lessons,* p. 69.

"It is not for your sake, you Israelites, that I am acting, but for the sake of my holy name. . . . I will hallow my great name, which has been profaned among those nations. When they see that *I reveal my holiness through you,* the nations will know that I am the LORD, says the Lord God" (Eze. 36: 22, 23, N.E.B.).

We must not fail Him!

When the Christian "Misses the Mark"

WE MET our imaginary man, John, in chapter six, and since then have gotten to know him fairly well. When we met him he was at a low ebb, spiritually. For, although he was a church member "in good and regular standing," he had many habits and attitudes that told us he was not really a Christian.

Then we watched him as the Holy Spirit was able to get through to him and he began to respond. We saw him give up more and more of his sinful habits and practices until he had *almost* surrendered totally to the wooings of God.

We witnessed self putting up a stiff battle and finally, sadly, watched John give way and, as a result, slide back to his old, comfortable manner of life, in which he could still be an apparently good church member, but was far from his God.

In chapter ten we went "in depth" into John's experience, as it were, and analyzed the faculties involved in his struggle. We saw reason and judgment tell him he ought to surrender to the Holy Spirit's invitations. We described how desires and feelings strenuously objected to that step. And we decided that the struggle could be resolved in only one way: by an action of John's will.

In this chapter let's think about John one more time. Suppose that, on another occasion, the Spirit comes to him in a constraining manner. Again John is faced with his sins, external and internal. Again reason and desires wrestle with each other. But this time John places his will decisively on the side of reason and right. He surrenders self totally to God, and thus is released from the bondage of sin.

When this happens, John enters into a relationship with Christ that entirely changes his standing with God and his feelings toward God. Theologically, this is called justification.

Justification, as we have just intimated, has two aspects. The first may be termed legal, the second, experiential. In the first we may think in terms of a court in which the penalty of the guilty prisoner has been paid, and therefore there is no longer any charge against him. So Christ has paid the penalty for the sinner who accepts Him and gives himself to Him. Therefore the sinner stands before God as if he had never sinned.

> If you give yourself to Him [Christ], and accept Him as your Saviour, then, sinful as your life may have been, for His sake you are accounted righteous. Christ's character stands in place of your character, and you are accepted before God just as if you had not sinned.—*Steps to Christ*, p. 62.

Justification is sometimes explained as nothing more than a legal transaction by which sins recorded in the books of heaven are canceled after one accepts the fact that Jesus is Saviour, and confesses his sins. But there is another vitally important element required, without which, in fact, one is not justified.

> Justification is given only to those who accept and commit themselves to God's whole plan of righteousness by faith in Christ.—*The SDA Bible Commentary*, vol. 6, p. 521.
>
> God requires the entire surrender of the heart, before justification can take place.—*Selected Messages*, book 1, p. 366.
>
> Forgiveness [an aspect of justification] has a broader meaning than many suppose. . . . God's forgiveness is not merely a judicial act by which He sets us free from condemnation. It is not only forgiveness *for* sin, but reclaiming *from* sin. It is the outflow of redeeming love that transforms the heart.—*Thoughts From the Mount of Blessing*, p. 114.

A Change in Mental Posture

The second aspect of justification, then, the experiential aspect, begins in John with a change of mental posture caused by the Holy Spirit's coming into his life and transforming his attitude. This is what Paul is writing about in Romans 12:2: "Be ye transformed by the renewing of your mind."

This radical change of attitude brings John into sympathy and agreement with God, and produces peace in the soul. "Therefore being justified by faith, we have peace with God through our Lord Jesus Christ" (chap. 5:1). "And the peace of God, which passeth all understanding, shall keep your hearts and minds through Christ Jesus" (Phil. 4:7).

This experience of the born-again Christian may be illustrated by that marvelous mechanical device called a gyroscope that is used to stabilize ships and planes, and is used in many other situations where stability and equilibrium are required. The device, which seems to defy gravity, keeps its balance despite counter influences. This is because of a rapidly spinning wheel, which tends to remain in its initial position. This tendency may be demonstrated by a toy gyroscope in operation. Try to push it gently from its position, and it persists in holding that position.

If you point the axle of a rapidly spinning gyroscope at the sun the end of the axle will appear to follow the sun as it makes its way across the sky. This is because the gyroscope maintains its original position in space while the earth turns beneath it.

How beautifully this illustrates the experience of the justified person. One aspect of this is described in *The Desire of Ages* in these words:

> Those who take Christ at His word, and surrender their souls to His keeping, their lives to His ordering, will find peace and quietude. Nothing of the world can make them sad when Jesus makes them glad by His presence.—Page 331.

Jesus' dwelling within is like a spiritual gyroscope that keeps us at peace although all around us may be moving in another direction, and seeking to push us in another direction.

Space vehicles, such as *Mariner I* and *II*, had gyroscopes set for horizontal, vertical, and transverse control, so that every possible movement was under gyroscopic control. Should some situation tend to cause deviation from the course to which they were locked, the gyroscopes would offset the interference.

The born-again Christian has similar spiritual "gyroscopic controls" that are meant to keep him from going off course: "Thine ears shall hear a word behind thee, saying, This is the way, walk ye in it, when ye turn to the right hand, and when ye turn to the left" (Isa. 30:21).

Our subject, John, then, has surrendered to Christ, sin has been expelled from the soul, guilt has been removed, the Holy Spirit dwells within; he has spiritual stability and equilibrium. Can he now expect that he will not again be troubled by sin; that he is now immune to sin and sinning?

The answer, we realize, is No. No more than a plane or ship can expect that no forces will operate to get it off course when it is fitted with gyroscopes. We have just discussed this matter in the foregoing chapter. For example, we considered the statement: "As long as Satan reigns we shall have self to subdue, besetments to overcome, and there is no stopping place."—*My Life Today*, p. 249.

Justification Does Not Destroy Self

Justification and the new birth, then, do not destroy self, which concept is explained in the allegory of the previous chapter and chapter 6. They do remove it from the throne of the life, and make available needed resources to defeat it.[84]

But while John cannot expect to escape being troubled by self and sin, at the same time God's ideal for him is that he no longer be overcome by them. "My little children," writes the apostle John, "these things write I unto you that ye sin not." But then he continues, "And if any man sin, we have an advocate with the Father, Jesus Christ the righteous" (1 John 2:1).

The Greek word here translated sin is *hamartia,* which means, missing the mark. Thus sin is missing the mark that God has set for us, which mark is a character that parallels the life our Saviour lived as a man by obeying His Father completely.[85]

One may miss the mark in two ways—willingly, deliberately, or unwillingly, unintentionally. The born-again person does not sin intentionally, willingly.

140

When the Christian "Misses the Mark"

When we are clothed with the righteousness of Christ, we shall have no relish for sin; for Christ will be working with us. We may make mistakes, but we will hate the sin that caused the sufferings of the Son of God.—*Selected Messages*, book 1, p. 360.

We shall fail often in our efforts to copy the divine pattern. We shall often have to bow down to weep at the feet of Jesus, because of our shortcomings and mistakes; but we are not to be discouraged; we are to pray more fervently, believe more fully, and try again with more steadfastness to grow into the likeness of our Lord. —*Ibid.*, p. 337.

This brings us to an important question: If the born-again person may have complete victory over sin and self, why is it that he sometimes fails? Or, to get back to our gyroscope illustration, if the axle of the spiritual gyroscope is set on the Sun of Righteousness, how does it get nudged off course?

A number of answers may be given to this question.

One is that the Christian's faith may temporarily falter. Such was the case with Elijah after his great triumph over the prophets of Baal on Mount Carmel (1 Kings 18, 19).

Integrally linked with this is the fact that the Christian sometimes takes his eyes off Jesus. In her discussion of Peter's failure after beginning to walk on the water, Ellen White says:

When trouble comes upon us, how often we are like Peter! We look upon the waves, instead of keeping our eyes fixed upon the Saviour. Our footsteps slide, and the proud waters go over our souls.—*The Desire of Ages*, p. 382.

Neglected Prayer and Study

An important reason that we lose sight of Jesus is that we do not spend time in thoughtful meditation and prayer, and in the study of the Word.

Then, Satan may temporarily succeed in getting the Christian to forget the Lord. He may so succeed in focusing his attention on his problems that he fails to remember Him who is the solution to them. The adversary "knows that if he can obscure our vision, so that the eye of faith cannot see God, there will be no barrier against sin" (*Thoughts From the Mount of Blessing*, p. 92). "Too often we forget the Lord. Self gives way to impulse, and we lose the victories that we should gain."—*God's Amazing Grace*, p. 179.

Still another reason that the Christian may temporarily fail is that he permits self and sin to assert itself briefly. Envy, pride, self-righteousness, anger, or some other besetment may rise to the surface and find expression.[86] Or one of them may show itself so suddenly that the Christian is caught off guard, and fails. This may especially be the experience of the Christian who is new in the way and in whom the habit patterns we referred to in the last chapter are still deep. But he must not become discouraged because of this.

Some earnest Christians fear that when they fail under these circumstances they are separated from God. Let them ponder these encouraging words:

> If one who daily communes with God errs from the path, if he turns a moment from looking steadfastly unto Jesus, it is not because he sins willfully; for when he sees his mistake, he turns again, and fastens his eyes upon Jesus [his spiritual gyroscope brings him back to position], and the fact that he has erred, does not make him less dear to the heart of God.—*Review and Herald,* May 12, 1896.

However, it is well to realize that,

> the willful commission of a known sin silences the witnessing voice of the Spirit and separates the soul from God.—*The Sanctified Life,* p. 92.

How Character Is Revealed

We may also remember that "the character is revealed, not by occasional good deeds and occasional [unintentional] misdeeds, but by the tendency of the habitual words and acts."— *Steps to Christ,* pp. 57, 58.

> If you have made mistakes, you certainly gain a victory if you see these mistakes and regard them as beacons of warning. Thus you turn defeat into victory, disappointing the enemy and honoring your Redeemer.—*Christ's Object Lessons,* p. 332.

When the Christian recognizes his mistakes, turns immediately from them, repents and confesses, is aware of his own great weakness and the need of a greater dependence upon his Saviour, he has gained a victory and prepared himself for future victories.

The question is sometimes asked, You say that the born-again person, in his battle with sin, is sometimes overcome. If this is so, what is the difference between him and the unregenerate person, the church member who is not born again, but who also struggles with sin and fails as the born-again person does?

Remember the gyroscope? As soon as a ship equipped with the device is hit by a wave, immediately the gyroscope is at work to maintain the ship's balance. So with the born-again person. When any weakness or temptation tends to cause him to sin, his spiritual gyroscope, the new heart that is set toward God, operates to bring him back in balance.

The person who is not born again does not have this stabilizer. It is a case of "the good that I would I do not: but the evil which I would not, that I do" (Rom. 7:19). So he struggles to maintain his spiritual equilibrium against sin and self. But he cannot keep it. He does not have a gyroscope.

Remember, also, that this stability in the born-again person that is seen outwardly, operates inwardly. It is the result of the renewed heart and mind guided by the Holy Spirit. The unregenerate may sometimes manage to maintain an outward appearance of victory, when inwardly he is far off center. But he whose life is in Jesus has victory within. When he turns to Jesus for aid, his feeling of anger, or resentment, or envy, dies. He is at peace. In the unregenerate the feeling continues to seethe, and he may later take it out on his wife, or children, or someone else.

The way of the born-again person then, is the way of victory, inwardly and outwardly, even though defeat may sometimes seem to be his lot. For the fact that he turns his eyes toward Jesus when sin intrudes, means that, by the very act of turning, he has changed a momentary setback into a victory.

Focus on Victory

PETER had a problem. Peter, the disciple of Jesus, that is. Peter frequently had problems, but this particular one had to do with forgiveness. How many times should one forgive a person who has wronged him? Some believe the rabbis limited it to three. But Peter had had enough to do with Jesus to know He would go beyond that. Considering the question, the disciple concluded that his Master would probably go to the perfect number seven. He decided to check out his idea.

"Lord, how often shall my brother sin against me, and I forgive him? As many as seven times?" he asked (Matt. 18:21, R.S.V.).

Jesus' answer must have chagrined Peter. "I do not say to you seven times, but seventy times seven."

What Jesus was saying, in essence, was, There must be no end to the number of times you are willing to forgive. God's willingness to forgive knows no limits; yours must know no limits.

This we all understand. This is marvelous! But it brings to mind another problem.

Here are two friends, George and Jim. One day Jim comes to George and says, "George, I owe you an apology. Yesterday, when we were discussing that problem about overtime work, I sort of lost my temper. I'm sorry. Will you forgive me?"

And George generously forgives.

A few days later Jim comes to George again. "Say, George, it was stupid of me to take the attitude I did last night. And on top of it I lost my cool. I'm sorry. Please forgive me."

In about a week another situation arises in which Jim gets heated up, and afterward feels it necessary to ask George's forgiveness. A few days later something else happens, and Jim, very shamefacedly, must apologize once more and ask forgiveness.

And so it goes. Every little while Jim loses his temper with George. Then, because he is basically a decent fellow, and because he wants to retain George's friendship, and because he is trying to be a Christian, he apologizes and asks forgiveness. And always, without any reservation, kindhearted George happily forgives, and puts the whole thing from his mind. Fine!

But how about Jim? What is his problem doing with his morale, his self-respect, for example? Doesn't it go down a notch every time he has to apologize? Doesn't he begin to feel very weak, morally?

The Effects of Defeat

Chronic defeat is a terribly demoralizing thing. The most optimistic, the most courageous, the most tenacious, can't go on forever being defeated. There has to be meaningful victory sometimes.

And consider how Jim gets to feel as time after time he is constrained to go to George and ask forgiveness. Embarrassed? In fact, after a time he certainly begins to avoid George, because he can't put up with having to keep asking for his forgiveness.

In some respects our illustration may be overdrawn. In other ways it is not. For while God will freely forgive seventy times seven and seven hundred times seven, there is the factor of shame, defeatism, and other attitudes that must dog the sincere Christian who keeps failing on the score of a particular weakness year after year, as was suggested in chapter eight.

In fact, there is something lacking if we continue to need to go to God year after year, seeking pardon for the same particular sin. His pardon "is not only forgiveness *for* sin, but

10

reclaiming *from* sin" *(Thoughts From the Mount of Blessing,* p. 114).

In the *Review and Herald* of April 21, 1891, Ellen White asks in a sermon, in a way that suggests a situation that ought not to be, "Are there those here who have been sinning [the same sins] and repenting, sinning and repenting, and will they continue to do so till Christ shall come?"

This book is about Christian victory. In most of the chapters we have endeavored to describe as clearly as we know how, ways by which we may gain the victory over sin and Satan. But in this chapter we want to focus on, and fortify, the idea of Christian victory.

There is surely great significance in the fact that, in His messages to the seven churches (Revelation 3, 4), Christ's rewards are only for him "that overcometh." In the case of every one of the churches this proviso is made. In the Bible there is no provision made for defeat. Only victors will stand on the sea of glass, partake of the tree of life, and live eternally with Christ.

Defeat Is Unnecessary

No allowance is made for defeat, because there is no necessity for defeat.

> We can overcome. Yes; fully, entirely. Jesus died to make a way of escape for us, that we might overcome every evil temper, every sin, every temptation, and sit down at last with Him.—*Testimonies,* vol. 1, p. 144.
>
> Every provision has been made for us to receive divine power, which will enable us to overcome temptation.—*General Conference Bulletin,* 1899, p. 99.
>
> The life that Christ lived in this world, men and women can live through His power and under His instruction. In their conflict with Satan they may have all the help that He had.—*Testimonies,* vol. 9, pp. 21, 22.

We ended chapter eight with a drawing of a heart with the name "Christ" inside, to represent the born-again person, the new life in which there are new motives, desires, inclinations, and attitudes.

Let us add something to this that clarifies why we may have victory:

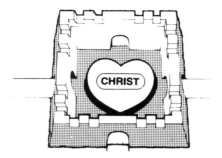

"We know that no child of God is a [habitual] sinner; it is the Son of God who keeps him safe, and the evil one cannot touch him" (1 John 5:18, N.E.B.).[87]

> The soul that is yielded to Christ becomes His own fortress . . . in a revolted world, and He intends that no authority shall be known in it but His own. A soul thus kept in possession by the heavenly agencies is impregnable to the assaults of Satan. . . . The only defense against evil is the indwelling of Christ in the heart through faith in His righteousness.—*The Desire of Ages,* p. 324.

> By yielding up your will to Christ, your life will be hid with Christ in God and allied to the power which is above all principalities and powers. You will have strength from God that will hold you fast to His strength. . . . But your will must co-operate with God's will.—*Testimonies,* vol. 5, p. 514.

Victory, then, is a work of cooperation. But the responsibilities are not equal. In fact—

> The part man is required to sustain is *immeasurably small,* yet in the plan of God it is just that part that is needed to make the work a success. . . . The co-operation of the human will and endeavor with divine energy is the link that binds men up with one another and with God.—Manuscript 113, Sept. 8, 1898. (Italics supplied.)

> The work of the Holy Spirit is immeasurably great.—*Review and Herald,* Nov. 29, 1892.

> There is great necessity for us to realize our dependence on God. Too much confidence is placed in man, too much reliance on human inventions. There is too little confidence in the power which God stands ready to give. . . . *Immeasurably inferior* is the part which the human agent sustains; but if he is linked with the divinity of Christ, he can do all things through the strength that Christ imparts. —*Christ's Object Lessons,* p. 82. (Italics supplied.)

In these statements is a vital key to Christian victory. Not

147

How to Be a Victorious Christian

by our own efforts, not in our own strength, not by our own knowledge or wisdom, is victory gained. The victory is won as moment by moment by faith we depend upon Christ's power. For, in the battle with sin, our strength, whatever we may think, is as a straw trying to control a hurricane.

Our Greatest Struggle

In the battle of life our greatest struggle will not be to overcome sin, but to surrender self.

> Some who come to God by repentance and confession, and even believe that their sins are forgiven, still fail of claiming, as they should, the promises of God. . . . They are not ready to commit the keeping of their souls to Him [Jesus], relying upon Him to perfect the work of grace begun in their hearts. While they think they are committing themselves to God, there is a great deal of self-dependence. There are conscientious souls that trust partly to God, and partly to themselves. They do not look to God, to be kept by His power, but depend upon watchfulness against temptation, and the performance of certain duties for acceptance with Him. *There are no victories in this kind of faith.—Selected Messages,* book 1, p. 353. (Italics supplied.)
> If we do not choose to give ourselves fully to God, then we are in darkness. When we make any reserve, we are leaving open a door [visualize the fortress around the heart] through which Satan can enter to lead us astray by his temptations. He knows that if he can obscure our vision, so that the eye of faith cannot see God, there will be no barrier against sin.—*Thoughts From the Mount of Blessing,* p. 92.

Now, be encouraged by these words: "Victory is sure when self is surrendered to God."—*The SDA Bible Commentary,* Ellen G. White Comments, on Gen. 32:24, p. 1095.

Here is a great truth that every *victorious* Christian has firmly grasped. He is not like a beleaguered soldier standing on a knoll surrounded by enemies besetting him on every hand, and occasionally receiving help from Christ. Instead, he is a soldier inside the strong fortress of God's love and grace. His task is to use the strength Christ has given him to assure that no enemy enters the gates. The walls are kept by Christ, and no enemy can breach them. "We are secure, perfectly secure from the enemy's subtlety while we have unwavering trust in God."—*Our High Calling,* p. 22.

As we have been emphasizing throughout this book, the

148

cornerstone of Christian victory is a perfect commitment to Christ—surrender. This surrender means giving over every area of life to God to be changed, purified, strengthened, as He wills.

Victories to Be Gained

It is not an easy matter to give up the rights of self in this way. But it is essential. This surrendering will mean a struggle with appetite for many.* For this area in which Eve was overcome is used with great success by Satan in bringing about the downfall of multitudes.

> The controlling power of appetite will prove the ruin of thousands, when, if they had conquered on this point, they would have had moral power to gain the victory over every other temptation of Satan. But those who are slaves to appetite will fail in perfecting Christian character.—*Testimonies*, vol. 3, pp. 491, 492.
>
> We need to learn that indulged appetite is the greatest hindrance to mental improvement and soul sanctification.—*Ibid.*, vol. 9, p. 156.

Another area of our lives where many need to gain decided victories is in the area of amusements. Amusements have become almost the sum total of interest in the lives of multitudes, not a few of whom are professing Christians. But the Christian, whose goal is heaven and a character that will be fit for heaven, cannot permit himself to become immersed in the types of entertainment common to the world—sports, the movies and TV, and certain other pastimes that wean the mind from Jesus.

> The powers of Satan are at work to keep minds diverted from eternal realities. The enemy has arranged matters to suit his own purposes. Worldly business, sports, the fashions of the day—these things occupy the minds of men and women.—*Ibid.*, p. 43.
>
> The only safe amusements are such as will not banish serious and religious thoughts; the only safe places of resort are those to which we can take Jesus with us.—*Our High Calling*, p. 284.

Other areas may be mentioned:

> Fashion is deteriorating the intellect and eating out the spirituality of our people. . . . And [it] is doing more than any other power to separate our people from God.—*Testimonies*, vol. 4, p. 647.

To make real victory possible means making everything

149

right with our fellow men, as well as with God. When the tax collector, Zacchaeus, said to Jesus, "Lord, . . . if I have defrauded any one of anything, I restore it fourfold," Jesus said, "Today salvation has come to this house" (Luke 19:8, 9, R.S.V.).

Alluding to Ezekiel 33:15, which discusses restitution to ones wronged,[89] Ellen White says—

> There is no evidence of genuine repentance, unless it works reformation. If he restore the pledge, give again that he had robbed, confess his sins, and love God and his fellow men, the sinner may be sure that he has passed from death unto life.—*Steps to Christ,* p. 59.

Additional to the *requirement* for making restitution is another vital aspect, a clear conscience. No person can have such a conscience before himself and God until he has made restitution for every known sin. And no person can have a buoyant, confident, victorious experience while he has an accusing conscience.

Too Many Gates to Watch?

The price of Christian victory may seem too hard, too all-encompassing, too detailed, too demanding, for many. There may seem to be too many things to remember, too many gates to watch, as it were. But the problem is in the seeming more than in actuality when one is fully, unreservedly committed to Jesus. "When the tree is dead, the leaves fall off."

> The surrender of all our powers to God greatly simplifies the problem of life. It weakens and cuts short a thousand struggles with the passions of the natural heart. Religion is as a golden cord that binds the souls of both youth and aged to Christ. Through it the willing and obedient are brought safely through dark and intricate paths to the city of God.—*My Life Today,* p. 6.

There is another element absolutely vital to victory—perseverance.[90] "When you are in any contest," said Dwight D. Eisenhower, "you should work as if there were—to the very last minute—a chance to lose it. This is battle, this is politics, this is everything." It certainly is the Christian life! "He that shall endure unto the end, the same shall be saved," said Christ (Mark 13:13).

Revelation 14:12 is a text that Seventh-day Adventists feel

has a message for them in a special way. It comes at the close of the three angels' messages, which allude to the fearful struggle God's people will have with the beast and his image. The King James Version translation is the most familiar one to those Adventists whose language is English: "Here is the patience of the saints: here are they that keep the commandments of God, and the faith of Jesus."

The Greek term from which the word "patience" is translated is better rendered "steadfast endurance." The *New American Standard Bible* has, "Here is the perseverance of the saints."

Picture, then, a people who, under all the pressures of being accounted outlaws, of being cut off, from the human viewpoint, from every necessity of life, and finally of being sentenced to death, yet hold without wavering in their loyalty to God and His law.

> The season of distress and anguish before us will require a faith that can endure weariness, delay, and hunger,—a faith that will not faint though severely tried. The period of probation is granted to all to prepare for that time. Jacob prevailed because he was persevering and determined. His victory is an evidence of the power of importunate prayer. All who will lay hold of God's promises, as he did, and be as earnest and persevering as he was, will succeed as he succeeded.—*The Great Controversy,* p. 621.

There is another attitude assumed by some professed Christians that, unless radically resisted, will keep them from the joys of victory and life eternal:

> [Some] for a time are successful in the struggle against their selfish desire for pleasure and ease. They are sincere and earnest, but grow weary of protracted effort, of daily death, of ceaseless turmoil. Indolence seems inviting, death to self repulsive; and they close their drowsy eyes and fall under the power of temptation instead of resisting it.—*The Acts of the Apostles,* p. 565.

"So let us never tire of doing good, for if we do not slacken our efforts we shall in due time reap our harvest" (Gal. 6:9, N.E.B.). "His [the Lamb's] victory will be shared by his followers, called and chosen and *faithful*" (Rev. 17:14, N.E.B.).

Ere the Gates Close

AT SUNSET the gates of the city would close. Anxiously, the hurrying traveler noted the lowering sun. The distance he had to travel was greater than he had realized, and he had been delayed longer than he had planned for.

But he *had* to get to the city before the gates were barred. To remain outside the walls during the night was unthinkable. Vicious animals roamed in the darkness. And even more vicious men—robbers and murderers. Besides, the traveler was carrying with him all the money he owned, the savings of a lifetime. He *had* to get to the city before the gates closed. He dared not stop. There was too much at stake.

The reader can perhaps identify with the situation in which many an ancient traveler found himself. For, in some manner, and at some time, he too has toiled to reach his gates-about-to-close.

The gates we have been writing about in this volume are the gates of salvation and eternity. And, as Seventh-day Adventists, we know that soon, with a terrible finality, they will close silently, unrecognized, upon the world and the church.

There is a solemn, eloquent passage in *The Desire of Ages* to which we frequently turn when we wish to emphasize the heedlessness of the world as probation closes:

> The crisis is stealing gradually upon us. The sun shines in the heavens, passing over its usual round, and the heavens still declare

the glory of God. Men are still eating and drinking, planting and building, marrying, and giving in marriage. Merchants are still buying and selling. Men are jostling one against another, contending for the highest place. . . . Yet probation's hour is fast closing, and every case is about to be eternally decided. Satan sees that his time is short. He has set all his agencies at work that men may be deceived, deluded, occupied and entranced, until the day of probation shall be ended, and the door of mercy forever shut.—Page 636.

Perhaps we are inclined to apply these words to the worldling, or to professed Christians in other churches where religion is but a formality. But they could be applied just as truly to some Seventh-day Adventists. Business and pleasure and the routine of life may sadly absorb some of us—many of us—so that we too may be caught outside the gates when it is too late.[91]

The Guideposts Are Up

But none need be. The guideposts are up and clearly marked. We have the maps—the Bible and Spirit of Prophecy writings. We can tell by these that the road of history is ending. We know that the day is drawing to a close, that there is not much time left.

There are some who think they are on the right road, who are not. Occasionally, they are beset by doubts as to the route they are taking, but they shake them off and press on.

Each of us, with the last rays of the sun of earth's day falling upon us, must know whether he is really on the road to heaven. It is not enough to *think* we are, to *hope* we are. We must *know!* We *must* be on the right road. And we must not linger a moment. For the sun has touched the western horizon. Perhaps already the appointed angel is winging his way to the gates to swing them forever shut. Perhaps, even now, Jesus instructs the angel to hold the gates a moment longer. Visualize Him watching, hopefully, for those He longs to see enter who have not entered. Lovingly, He stretches out His arms in yearning invitation. Urgently He calls, "Come, come, for all things are ready!"

Let us haste—ere the gates close.

Postscript

One of the great dangers, perhaps the greatest, threatening us as Christians is fade-out. God brings a message to us that shakes us awake to the perils of our situation, and drives home the need of immediate and drastic action. And we determine we will take action.

But soon the force of the impact wears off, the sense of urgency fades, and we fall back into spiritual slumber.

When probation closes, many Seventh-day Adventists will be found in this condition who genuinely meant to do something about it—but never did.

"Listen! *This* is the hour to receive God's favor, *today* is the day to be saved!" (2 Cor. 6:2, T.E.V.). Today and today and today we must be alert and ready, regardless of all things else, "for in such an hour as ye think not the Son of man cometh."

APPENDIX

RELEVANT QUOTATIONS FROM THE
SPIRIT OF PROPHECY WRITINGS

Perspective and Objective

[1] The necessity of experimental religion must be urged upon those who accept the theory of the truth. . . . All must obtain a living experience for themselves; they must have Christ enshrined in the heart, His Spirit controlling the affections, or their profession of faith is of no value, and their condition will be even worse than if they had never heard the truth.—*Testimonies,* vol. 5, p. 619.

[2] I speak plainly [wrote Ellen White]. I do not think this will discourage a true Christian; and I do not want any of you to come up to the time of trouble without a well-grounded hope in your Redeemer.—*Ibid.,* vol. 1, p. 163.

Willard Saxby and the Laodiceans

[3] The hope of eternal life is not to be received upon slight grounds. It is a subject to be settled between God and your own soul—settled for eternity. A supposed hope, and nothing more, will prove your ruin. Since you are to stand or fall by the word of God, it is to that word you must look for testimony in your case. There you can see what is required of you to become a Christian. Do not lay off your armor, or leave the battlefield until you have obtained the victory, and triumphed in your Redeemer.—*Ibid.,* pp. 163, 164.

[4] Many who think themselves Christians will at last be found wanting.—*Christ's Object Lessons,* p. 72.

[5] As many are today, so (before his conversion) Paul was very confident in an hereditary piety; but his confidence was founded on falsehood.—*Selected Messages,* book 1, p. 346.

The Irreducible Minimum

[6] True conviction of sin, real heart sorrow because of wickedness, death to self, the daily overcoming of defects of character, and the new birth. . . . Such a work many know nothing of. They grafted the truth into their natural hearts, and then went on as before, manifesting the same unhappy traits of character.—*Review and Herald,* Aug. 28, 1879.

[7] Regeneration is the only path by which we can enter the city of God. It is narrow, and the gate by which we enter is straight; but along it we are to lead men and women and children, teaching them that, in order to be saved, they must have a new heart and a new spirit. The old, hereditary traits of character must be overcome. The natural desires of the soul must be changed. . . . The new life, which makes men and women Christlike, is to be lived.—*Testimonies*, vol. 9, p. 23.

[8] Search carefully and see whether the truth which you have accepted has, with you, become a firm principle. Do you take Christ with you when you leave the closet of prayer? Does your religion stand guard at the door of your lips? Is your heart drawn out in sympathy and love for others outside of your own family? Are you diligently seeking a clearer understanding of scriptural truth, that you may let your light shine forth to others? These questions you may answer to your own souls.—*Review and Herald*, Jan. 8, 1880.

[9] [When one is justified] there is nothing in the heart at war with God's requirements. The mind, submissive and obedient, will love to do all His commandments. Evil will be abhorred, and the good will be chosen. There will be no self-denial or self-sacrifice that is grievous, for the heart delights in doing for Christ, and seeking to save souls from error and from the transgression of the holy law of God. When God has control of the affections, the mind will not be selfish, nor shrink from sacrifice.—*Ibid.*, Dec. 2, 1875.

[10] When Christ reigns in the soul, there is purity, freedom from sin. . . . The acceptance of the Saviour brings a glow of perfect peace, perfect love, perfect assurance.—*Christ's Object Lessons*, p. 420.

[11] Christ's love is deep and earnest, flowing like an irrepressible stream to all who will accept it. There is no selfishness in His love. If this heaven-born love is an abiding principle in the heart, it will make itself known, not only to those we hold most dear in sacred relationship, but to all with whom we come in contact. It will lead us to bestow little acts of attention, to make concessions, to perform deeds of kindness, to speak tender, true, encouraging words. It will lead us to sympathize with those whose hearts hunger for sympathy.—*The SDA Bible Commentary*, Ellen G. White Comments, on John 13:34, p. 1140.

[12] Many today assert their loyalty to God, but their concerts and other pleasure gatherings, their worldly associations, their glorifying of self, and their eager desire for popularity all testify that they have not obeyed His voice.—*Testimonies*, vol. 5, p. 88.

[13] God requires of His people now as great a distinction from the world, in customs, habits, and principles, as He required of Israel anciently. If they faithfully follow the teachings of His word, this distinction will exist; it cannot be otherwise.—*Patriarchs and Prophets*, p. 458.

[14] By what means shall we determine whose side we are on? Who has the heart? With whom are our thoughts? Upon whom do we love to converse? Who has our warmest affections and our best energies? If we are

on the Lord's side, our thoughts are with Him, and our sweetest thoughts are of Him. We have no friendship with the world; we have consecrated all that we have and are to Him. We long to bear His image, breathe His Spirit, do His will, and please Him in all things.—*Testimonies,* vol. 2, p. 262.

trivial [15] He who is drawing his life from Christ will have no desire for the frivolous, unsatisfying enjoyments of the world.—*Ibid.,* vol. 5, p. 88.

[16] We are to surrender ourselves to Him. When this surrender is entire, Christ can finish the work He began for us by the surrender of Himself. Then He can bring to us complete restoration.—*Review and Herald,* May 30, 1907.

[17] Those who are seeking the righteousness of Christ will be dwelling *Keeping the attention directed* upon the themes of the great salvation. The Bible is the storehouse that supplies their souls with nourishing food. They meditate upon the incarnation of Christ, they contemplate the great sacrifice made to save them from perdition, to bring in pardon, peace, and everlasting righteousness. The soul is aglow with these grand and elevating themes.—*Testimonies to Ministers,* pp. 87, 88.

[18] Sin not only shuts us away from God, but destroys in the human soul both the desire and the capacity for knowing Him. All this work of evil it is Christ's mission to undo. The faculties of the soul, paralyzed by sin, the darkened mind, the perverted will, He has power to invigorate and to restore.—*Education,* pp. 28, 29.

[19] The nearer we come to Jesus, and the more closely we discern the purity of His character, the more clearly shall we see the exceeding sinfulness of sin, and the less shall we feel like exalting ourselves.—*The Acts of the Apostles,* p. 561.

[20] Those who are justified by faith must have a heart to keep the way of the Lord. It is an evidence that a man is not justified by faith when his works do not correspond to his profession.—*Selected Messages,* book 1, p. 397.

The One Who Helps Us Cope

[21] If you have a sense of need in your soul, if you hunger and thirst after righteousness, this is an evidence that Christ has wrought upon your heart, in order that He may be sought unto to do for you, through the endowment of the Holy Spirit, those things which it is impossible for you to do for yourself.—*Thoughts From the Mount of Blessing,* p. 19.

[22] Christ died for all; and we are assured in His word that He is more willing to give His Holy Spirit to them that ask Him than are earthly parents to give good gifts to their children.—*The Sanctified Life,* p. 84.

The Heart of the Matter

[23] To man alone, the crowning work of His creation, God has given a conscience to realize the sacred claims of the divine law, and a heart capable of loving it as holy, just, and good; and of man prompt and per-

fect obedience is required.—*Selected Messages,* book 1, p. 216.

[24] The work of sanctification begins in the heart, and we must come into such a relation with God, that Jesus can put His divine mold upon us.—*Review and Herald,* Feb. 23, 1892.

[25] Christ gives man no encouragement to think that He will accept a patchwork character, made up mostly of self, with a little of Christ. This is the condition of the Laodicean church. At first there seems to be some of self and some of Christ. But soon it is all of self and none of Christ. . . . Christ looks with pitying tenderness on all who have combination characters. Those with such a character have a connection with Christ so frail that it is utterly worthless.—*The SDA Bible Commentary,* Ellen G. White Comments, on 2 Cor. 5:17, p. 1101.

[26] Only as we see our utter helplessness and renounce all self-trust, shall we lay hold on divine power. It is not only at the beginning of the Christian life that this renunciation of self is to be made. At every advance step heavenward it is to be renewed.—*The Ministry of Healing,* p. 455.

One-Hundred-Eighty-Degree Christians

[27] Often the question arises, Why . . . are there so many, claiming to believe God's word, in whom there is not seen a reformation in words, in spirit, and in character? Why are there so many who cannot bear opposition to their purposes and plans, who manifest an unholy temper, and whose words are harsh, overbearing, and passionate? There is seen in their lives the same love of self, the same selfish indulgence, the same temper and hasty speech, that is seen in the life of the worldling. There is the same sensitive pride, the same yielding to natural inclination, the same perversity of character, as if the truth were wholly unknown to them. The reason is that they are not converted.—*Christ's Object Lessons,* p. 99.

"If He Does Not Resist"

[28] If one sin is cherished in the soul, or one wrong practice retained in the life, the whole being is contaminated. The man becomes an instrument of unrighteousness.—*The Desire of Ages,* p. 313.

[29] Men want a dignified religion. They desire to walk in a path wide enough to take in their own attributes.—*Christ's Object Lessons,* p. 162.

[30] Every act of resistance makes it harder to yield.—*Testimonies to Ministers,* p. 74.

The Substance and Keynote of Jesus' Teaching

[31] The position all must come into, is to value salvation dearer than earthly gain, to count everything but loss that they may win Christ. The consecration must be entire. God will admit of no reserve, of no divided sacrifice, no idol. All must die to self, and to the world. Then let us each renew our consecration to God daily. Everlasting life is worth a life-

long, persevering, untiring effort.—*Review and Herald,* March 18, 1880.

[32] We are not God's children unless we are such entirely. There are those who profess to serve God, while they rely upon their own efforts to obey His law, to form a right character, and secure salvation. Their hearts are not moved by any deep sense of the love of Christ, but they seek to perform the duties of the Christian life as that which God requires of them in order to gain heaven. Such religion is worth nothing. When Christ dwells in the heart, the soul will be so filled with His love, with the joy of communion with Him, that it will cleave to Him; and in the contemplation of Him, self will be forgotten. Love to Christ will be the spring of action. . . . A profession of Christ without this deep love is mere talk, dry formality, and heavy drudgery.—*Steps to Christ,* pp. 44, 45.

[33] Many who profess to be Christ's followers have an anxious, troubled heart because they are afraid to trust themselves with God. They do not make a complete surrender to Him, for they shrink from the consequences that such a surrender may involve. Unless they do make this surrender they cannot find peace.—*The Ministry of Healing,* pp. 480, 481.

[34] God will not accept your offerings if you withhold yourself. He asks not only for that which is His own in the means intrusted to you, but for his own property in your body, soul, and spirit, purchased at the infinite price of the blood of the Son of God.—*Review and Herald,* Oct. 31, 1878.

[35] In heaven it is said by the ministering angels: The ministry which we have been commissioned to perform we have done. . . . [There follows a description of the angel's ministry.] Their [the sinners'] hearts were deeply moved by a sense of the sin that crucified the Son of God. They were convicted. They saw the steps to be taken in conversion; they felt the power of the gospel; their hearts were made tender as they saw the sweetness of the love of God. They beheld the beauty of the character of Christ. But with the many it was all in vain. They would not surrender their own habits and character. They would not put off the garments of earth in order to be clothed with the robe of heaven. Their hearts were given to covetousness. They loved the associations of the world more than they loved their God.—*Christ's Object Lessons,* p. 318.

[36] Not one nook or corner of the soul is to be a hiding place for selfishness.—*Testimonies,* vol. 8, pp. 139, 140.

[37] You cannot reach the full measure of the stature of Christ in a day, and you would sink in despair could you behold all the difficulties that must be met and overcome.—*Messages to Young People,* pp. 45, 46.

[38] All the elements of character which helped to make him successful and honored in the world,—the irrepressible desire for some greater good, the indomitable will, the strenuous exertion, the untiring perseverance,—are not to be crushed out. These are to remain, and through

11

the grace of God received into the heart, to be turned into another channel. These valuable traits of character may be exercised on objects as much higher and nobler than worldly pursuits as the heavens are higher than the earth.—*Review and Herald,* Oct. 25, 1881.

[39] While self is unsubdued we can find no rest. The masterful passions of the heart no human power can control.—*The Desire of Ages,* p. 336.

[40] But what do we give up, when we give all? A sin-polluted heart, for Jesus to purify, to cleanse by His own blood, and to save by His matchless love. And yet men think it hard to give up all!—*Steps to Christ,* p. 46.

[41] Every taxing duty becomes easy, and every sacrifice becomes a pleasure, to those whom the truth makes free. What a victory is gained when the carnal life ceases, and the spiritual life begins. . . . The mind, submissive and obedient, will love to do all His commandments. Evil will be abhorred, and the good will be chosen. There will be no self-denial . . . that is grievous, for the heart delights in doing for Christ, and seeking to save souls from error and from the transgression of the holy law of God. When God has control of the affections, the mind will not be selfish, nor shrink from sacrifices.—*Review and Herald,* Dec. 2, 1875.

But I Don't Want to Surrender!

[42] Sin not only shuts away from God, but destroys in the human soul both the desire and the capacity for knowing Him. Through sin, the whole human organism is deranged, the mind is perverted, the imagination corrupted; the faculties of the soul are degraded. . . . The soul is weak, and for want of moral force to overcome, is polluted and debased. —*Prophets and Kings,* p. 233.

[43] Repentance is thought to be a work the sinner must do for himself in order that he may come to Christ. They think that the sinner must procure for himself a fitness in order to obtain the blessing of God's grace. But while it is true that repentance must precede forgiveness, . . . the sinner cannot bring himself to repentance, or prepare himself to come to Christ. . . . The very first step to Christ is taken through the drawing of the Spirit of God; as man responds to this drawing, he advances toward Christ in order that he may repent.—*Selected Messages,* book 1, p. 390.

[44] I was shown God's people waiting for some change to take place,— a compelling power to take hold of them. But they will be disappointed, for they are wrong. They must act; they must take hold of the work themselves, and earnestly cry to God for a true knowledge of themselves. The scenes which are passing before us are of sufficient magnitude to cause us to arouse.—*Christian Service,* p. 43.

[45] It is by beholding His love, by dwelling upon it, by drinking it in, that we are to become partakers of His nature. What food is to the body, Christ must be to the soul. Food cannot benefit us unless we eat

it, unless it becomes a part of our being. So Christ is of no value to us if we do not know Him as a personal Saviour. A theoretical knowledge will do us no good.—*The Desire of Ages,* p. 389.

[46] The whole Bible is a manifestation of Christ. It is our only source of power.—*Gospel Workers,* p. 250.

[47] The reason that many professed Christians do not have a clear, well-defined experience, is that they do not think it is their privilege to understand what God has spoken through His word.—*Fundamentals of Christian Education,* p. 189.

[48] Those who study the word of God with hearts open to the enlightenment of the Holy Spirit, will not remain in darkness as to the meaning of the word. . . . All who come to Christ for a clearer knowledge of the truth will receive it. He will unfold to them the mysteries of the kingdom of heaven, and these mysteries will be understood by the heart that longs to know truth. A heavenly light will shine into the soul temple, and will be revealed to others as the bright shining of a lamp on a dark path.—*Christ's Object Lessons,* p. 36.

[49] The appreciation of the Bible grows with its study. Whichever way the student may turn, he will find displayed the infinite wisdom and love of God.—*Ibid.,* p. 132.

[50] It is a law both of the intellectual and spiritual nature that by beholding we become changed. The mind gradually adapts itself to the subjects upon which it is allowed to dwell. It becomes assimilated to that which it is accustomed to love and reverence.—*The Great Controversy,* p. 555.

The Soul's Controlling Faculty

[51] When we desire to be set free from sin, and in our great need cry out for a power out of and above ourselves, the powers of the soul are imbued with the divine energy of the Holy Spirit, and they obey the dictates of the will in fulfilling the will of God.—*The Desire of Ages,* p. 466.

[52] The result of the eating of the tree of knowledge of good and evil is manifest in every man's experience. There is in his nature a bent to evil, a force which, unaided, he cannot resist.—*Education,* p. 29.

[53] No man can be forced to transgress. His own consent must be first gained; the soul must purpose the sinful act before passion can dominate over reason or iniquity triumph over conscience. Temptation, however strong, is never an excuse for sin. . . . Cry unto the Lord, tempted soul. Cast yourself, helpless, unworthy, upon Jesus, and claim His very promise. The Lord will hear. He knows how strong are the inclinations of the natural heart, and He will help in every time of temptation.—*Testimonies,* vol. 5, p. 177.

Faith and an Orange

[54] God is able and willing to bestow upon His servants all the

strength they need and to give them the wisdom that their varied necessities demand. He will more than fulfill the highest expectations of those who put their trust in Him.—*The Acts of the Apostles,* p. 242.

A Question of Feelings

[55] There are those who if they feel they are not rightly used, become sour, ungenerous, crabbed and uncourteous in their words and deportment. They sink down discouraged, hateful and hating others.— *The SDA Bible Commentary,* Ellen G. White Comments, on Gen. 39:20, p. 1097.

[56] Satan attacks us at our weak points, but we need not be overcome. However severe or unexpected the assault, God has provided help for us, and in His strength we may conquer.—*Patriarchs and Prophets,* p. 421.

[57] When the grace of meekness is cherished by those who are naturally sour or hasty in disposition, they will put forth the most earnest efforts to subdue their unhappy temper. Every day they will gain self-control, until that which is unlovely and unlike Jesus is conquered. They become assimilated to the Divine Pattern, until they can obey the inspired injunction, "Be swift to hear, slow to speak, slow to wrath."—*Review and Herald,* Jan. 18, 1881.

[58] When depression settles upon the soul, it is no evidence that God has changed.—*Our High Calling,* p. 324.

[59] Many make a serious mistake in their religious life by keeping the attention fixed upon their feelings and thus judging of their advancement or decline. Feelings are not a safe criterion. We are not to look within for evidence of our acceptance with God. We shall find there nothing but that which will discourage us. Our only hope is in "looking unto Jesus." . . . There is everything in Him to inspire with hope, with faith, and with courage. He is our righteousness, our consolation and rejoicing.—*Testimonies,* vol. 5, pp. 199, 200.

Is Your Soul Breathing Properly?

[60] Neglect the exercise of prayer, or engage in prayer spasmodically, now and then, as seems convenient, and you lose your hold on God.— *Gospel Workers,* p. 255.

[61] We may commune with God in our hearts; we may walk in companionship with Christ. When engaged in our daily labor, we may breathe out our heart's desire, inaudible to any human ear; but that word cannot die away into silence, nor can it be lost. Nothing can drown the soul's desire. It rises above the din of the street, above the noise of machinery. It is God to whom we are speaking, and our prayer is heard. —*Ibid.,* p. 258.

[62] It is a lamentable fact that the erring heart is unwilling to be criticised, or to subject itself to humiliation by the confession of sin. Some see their faults, but thinking confession will detract from their dignity, they excuse their wrong, and shield themselves from the disci-

pline that confession would give to the soul.—*Fundamentals of Christian Education,* pp. 239, 240.

[63] To every sincere prayer an answer will come. It may not come just as you desire, or at the time you look for it; but it will come in the way and at the time that will best meet your need. The prayers you offer in loneliness, in weariness, in trial, God answers, not always according to your expectations, but always for your good.—*Gospel Workers* p. 258.

[64] God does not say, Ask once, and you shall receive. He bids us ask. Unwearyingly persist in prayer. The persistent asking brings the petitioner into a more earnest attitude, and gives him an increased desire to receive the things for which he asks.—*Christ's Object Lessons,* p. 145.

The Fourth Japanese Monkey

[65] The thoughts of the heart are discerned of God. When impure thoughts are cherished, they need not be expressed by word or act to consummate the sin and bring the soul into condemnation.—*Testimonies,* vol. 4, p. 623.

[66] An impure thought tolerated, an unholy desire cherished, and the soul is contaminated, its integrity compromised. "Then when lust hath conceived, it bringeth forth sin: and sin, when it is finished, bringeth forth death." If we would not commit sin, we must shun its very beginnings. Every emotion and desire must be held in subjection to reason and conscience. Every unholy thought must be instantly repelled.—*Ibid.,* vol. 5, p. 177.

[67] Satan tempted the first Adam in Eden, and Adam reasoned with the enemy, thus giving him the advantage.—*The SDA Bible Commentary,* Ellen G. White Comments, on Matt. 4:1-11, p. 1081.

[68] There are thoughts and feelings suggested . . . by Satan that annoy even the best of men; but if they are not cherished, if they are repulsed as hateful, the soul is not contaminated with guilt, and no other is defiled by their influence.—*Review and Herald,* March 27, 1888.

[69] When the mind has been long permitted to dwell only on earthly things, it is a difficult matter to change the habits of thought. That which the eye sees and the ear hears, too often attracts the attention and absorbs the interest. . . . The words and the character of Christ should be often the subject of our thoughts and of our conversation; and each day some time should be especially devoted to prayerful meditation upon these sacred themes.—*Ibid.,* May 3, 1881.

[70] If the professed people of God find their hearts opposed to this straight work, it should convince them that they have a work to do to overcome, if they would not be spewed out of the mouth of the Lord.—*Testimonies,* vol. 1, p. 187.

Two Fundamental Lessons

[71] The religion of Christ means more than the forgiveness of sin; it means taking away our sins, and filling the vacuum with the graces of

the Holy Spirit.—*Christ's Object Lessons*, pp. 419, 420.

⁷² All power is given into His [Christ's] hands, that He may dispense rich gifts unto men, *imparting* the priceless gift of His own righteousness to the helpless human agent. This is the message that God commanded to be given to the world. It is the third angel's message, which is to be proclaimed with a loud voice, and attended with the outpouring of His Spirit in a large measure.—*Testimonies to Ministers*, p. 92. (Italics supplied.)

Was Satan Right?

⁷³ Those who put their trust in Christ are not to be enslaved by any hereditary or cultivated habit or tendency. Instead of being held in bondage to the lower nature, they are to rule every appetite and passion. God has not left us to battle with evil in our own finite strength. Whatever may be our inherited or cultivated tendencies to wrong, we can overcome through the power that He is ready to impart.—*The Ministry of Healing*, pp. 175, 176.

⁷⁴ Let not anyone be afraid of going to extremes while he is a close student of the Word, humbling the soul at every step.—*Selected Messages*, book 2, p. 22.

Proving Satan Wrong

⁷⁵ The lower passions have their seat in the body and work through it. The words "flesh" or "fleshly" or "carnal lusts" embrace the lower, corrupt nature.—*The Adventist Home*, p. 127.

⁷⁶ When we have a realization of our weakness, we learn to depend upon a power not inherent. Nothing can take so strong a hold on the heart as the abiding sense of our responsibility to God. Nothing reaches so fully down to the deepest motives of conduct as a sense of the pardoning love of Christ. . . . While you look higher than yourself, you will have a continual sense of the weakness of humanity.—*The Desire of Ages*, p. 493.

⁷⁷ It is the Holy Spirit . . . that changes our character into the image of Christ; and when this is accomplished, we reflect, as in a mirror, the glory of the Lord. That is, the character of the one who thus beholds Christ is so like His, that one looking at him sees Christ's own character shining out as from a mirror. Imperceptibly to ourselves, we are changed day by day from our own ways and will into the ways and will of Christ, into the loveliness of His character. Thus we grow up into Christ, and unconsciously reflect His image.—*Review and Herald*, April 28, 1891.

⁷⁸ None can walk safely unless they are distrustful of self, and are constantly looking to the Word of God, studying it with willing heart to see their own errors, and to learn the will of Christ, and praying that it may be done in and by and through them. They show that their confidence is not in themselves, but in Christ.—*Our High Calling*, p. 212.

[79] He [man] . . . may progress in mental and moral dignity, until he reaches a perfection of intelligence and a purity of character but little lower than the perfection and purity of angels.—*Testimonies,* vol. 4, p. 93.

[80] Day by day he [Enoch] was growing away from his own way into Christ's way.—*Review and Herald,* April 28, 1891.

[81] Every moment that we are not on our watch we are liable to be beset by the enemy and are in great danger of being overcome by the powers of darkness. Satan commissions his angels to be vigilant and overthrow all they can; to find out the waywardness and besetting sins of those who profess the truth, and throw darkness around them, that they may cease to be watchful, take a course that will dishonor the cause they profess to love, and bring sorrow upon the church.—*Early Writings,* p. 105.

[82] There will be a people who hold so fast to the divine strength that they will be proof against every temptation.—*Sons and Daughters of God,* p. 143.

[83] This work [sanctification] can be accomplished only through faith in Christ, by the power of the indwelling Spirit of God. . . . The Christian will feel the promptings of sin, but he will maintain a constant warfare against it.—*The Great Controversy,* pp. 469, 470.

When the Christian "Misses the Mark"

[84] We can overcome. Yes; fully, entirely. Jesus died to make a way of escape for us, that we might overcome every evil temper, every sin, every temptation, and sit down at last with Him.—*Testimonies,* vol. 1, p. 144.

[85] If we will trust Him, and commit our ways to Him, He will direct our steps in the very path that will result in our obtaining the victory over every evil passion, and every trait of character that is unlike the character of our divine Pattern.—*Our High Calling,* p. 316.

[86] The servants of Christ are not to act out the dictates of the natural heart. They need to have close communion with God, lest, under provocation, self rise up, and they pour forth a torrent of words that are unbefitting, that are not as dew or the still showers that refresh the withering plants. This is what Satan wants them to do; for these are his methods. It is the dragon that is wroth; it is the spirit of Satan that is revealed in anger and accusing.—*The Desire of Ages,* p. 353.

Focus on Victory

[87] If we are determined not to be separated from the Source of our strength, Jesus will be just as determined to be at our right hand to help us, that we may not be put to shame before our enemies.—*Counsels on Health,* p. 424.

[88] We need to learn that indulged appetite is the greatest hindrance

to mental improvement and soul sanctification.—*Counsels on Diet and Foods,* p. 45.

[88] Let those who have committed wrong give proof of their repentance by seeking to make full restitution, let them in their after-life give evidence of a genuine reformation, and they will assuredly enjoy the peace of Heaven.—*Review and Herald,* Jan. 3, 1882.

[90] The work of salvation is not child's play, to be taken hold of at will and let alone at pleasure. It is the steady purpose, the untiring effort, that will gain the victory at last. It is he who endureth to the end that shall be saved.—*Testimonies,* vol. 2, pp. 101, 102.

Ere the Gates Close

[91] The powers of Satan are at work to keep minds diverted from eternal realities. The enemy has arranged matters to suit his own purposes. Worldly business, sports, the fashions of the day—these things occupy the minds of men and women.—*Ibid.,* vol. 9, p. 43.